CW01655409

CGP

GCSE Edexcel

Spanish

GCSE Spanish is a lot of fun but it also takes practice.

That's where this CGP Workbook comes in — it's full of exam-style questions to test you on reading, writing, listening and speaking, plus grammar practice to check you know your *ser* from your *estar*.

There's also lots of online practice in CGP RevisionHub — you'll find all the audio you need for the speaking and listening questions, plus model answer videos to help you get the most out of your revision. Grab your practice hat and get stuck in!

Unlock **CGP RevisionHub**

Just scan a QR code in the book to access the CGP RevisionHub.
Or go to **cgpbooks.co.uk/revise** and enter this code!

0831 8484 1195 5882

Revision Hub

By the way, this code only works for one person. If somebody else has used this book before you, they might have already claimed the code.

Exam Practice Workbook

with new **CGP RevisionHub**

Contents

How To Use This Book ... 1

Section One — General Stuff

Numbers, Times, Days and Dates ... 2
Questions and Being Polite ... 4
Opinions ... 6

Theme 1: My Personal World

Section Two — Identity and Relationships with Others

About Yourself and My Family & Friends ... 8
Describing People and Relationships ... 10
Role Models and Celebrations ... 12

Theme 2: Lifestyle and Wellbeing

Section Three — Healthy Living

Food ... 14
Physical & Mental Wellbeing and Illnesses & Treatments ... 16

Section Four — Free-time Activities

Music, Cinema and TV ... 18
Sports, Going Out and Other Hobbies ... 20

Themes 1 and 2 — Mixed Practice

Mixed Practice — Foundation ... 22
Mixed Practice — Both Tiers ... 26
Mixed Practice — Higher ... 28

Theme 3: My Neighbourhood

Section Five — Places in Town

Where You Live and At Home ... 32
The Local Area ... 34
Shopping, Directions and Weather ... 36

Section Six — Environmental and Social Issues

Environmental Problems, Effects and Protection ... 38
Equality and Social Issues ... 40

Theme 4: Media and Technology

Section Seven — Social Media and Technology

Technology, The Internet and Streaming ... 42
Social Media ... 44

Contents

Themes 3 and 4 — Mixed Practice

Mixed Practice — Foundation 46
Mixed Practice — Both Tiers 50
Mixed Practice — Higher 52

Theme 5: Studying and My Future

Section Eight — School

School Subjects and School Life 56
School Pressures and Difficulties 58

Section Nine — Future Opportunities

Education Post–16 and Career Choices & Ambitions 60

Theme 6: Travel and Tourism

Section Ten — Travel and Tourism

Where to Go and Accommodation & Travel 62
Tourist Attractions 64

Themes 5 and 6 — Mixed Practice

Mixed Practice — Foundation 66
Mixed Practice — Both Tiers 69
Mixed Practice — Higher 73

Grammar

Section Eleven — Nouns, Articles and Linking Words

Nouns and Articles 76
Pronouns 78
Prepositions and Conjunctions 80

Section Twelve — Adjectives and Adverbs

Adjectives 82
Adverbs 85
Quantifiers and Intensifiers 87

Section Thirteen — Verbs and Tenses

Present Tense 88
Past Tenses 90
The Future, The Conditional and Modal Verbs 92
Reflexives, '–ing' Verbs, Negatives and Impersonal Verbs 94
The Passive, Subjunctive and Imperative 96

Answers 98
Listening Transcripts 111
Speaking Transcripts 115

Published by CGP

Editors:
Siân Butler
Becca Clifford
Heather Cowley
Elliott Garraway
Brooke McCreight

With thanks to Encarna Aparicio-Dominguez, Lara Falomir Dominguez, Pollyanna Jackson and Hannah Roscoe for the proofreading.

With thanks to Robbie Driscoll for the copyright research.

Acknowledgements:
Audio produced by Voice Talent Online.

Questions throughout are based on Pearson Edexcel-type questions.

ISBN: 978 1 83774 199 1
Printed by Elanders Ltd, Newcastle upon Tyne.
Clipart from Corel®

Based on the classic CGP style created by Richard Parsons.
Text, design, layout and original illustrations © Coordination Group Publications Ltd. (CGP) 2025
All rights reserved.

Photocopying this book is not permitted, even if you have a CLA licence.
Extra copies are available from CGP with next day delivery • 0800 1712 712 • www.cgpbooks.co.uk

How To Use This Book

Step One: move those lovely eyeballs of yours over the collection of random squiggles on this page. Step Two: get brain to convert squiggles into words. Step Three: uncover the secrets to Spanish success.

This book follows the Edexcel specification

1) The content for Edexcel GCSE Spanish is divided into **six themes**.

My personal world	Lifestyle and wellbeing	My neighbourhood
Media and technology	Studying and my future	Travel and tourism

2) In this book, these six themes have been split into **ten sections**, with a section of mixed practice at the end of every two themes.
3) Section One covers **'General Stuff'**, with content that's useful across the course.
4) There are also three **grammar sections** that cover the grammar you need to know.

You can sit Higher or Foundation tier

1) You can choose to sit the **Higher-tier exams** or the **Foundation-tier exams**. You have to do the **same** tier for all four Spanish exams. Here are the main **differences** between them:
   - In **Foundation tier**, there's **less vocabulary** and **less grammar** to learn and the questions are slightly easier. In this tier, you can earn up to **Grade 5**.
   - In **Higher tier**, you can achieve **Grades 4-9**, but you'll need to learn **more vocab** and **more complex grammar**.
   - Speak to your **teacher** if you're not sure **which tier** you're sitting.
2) In this book, questions that are specific to one of the tiers have been marked up with a **bracket**, like this:

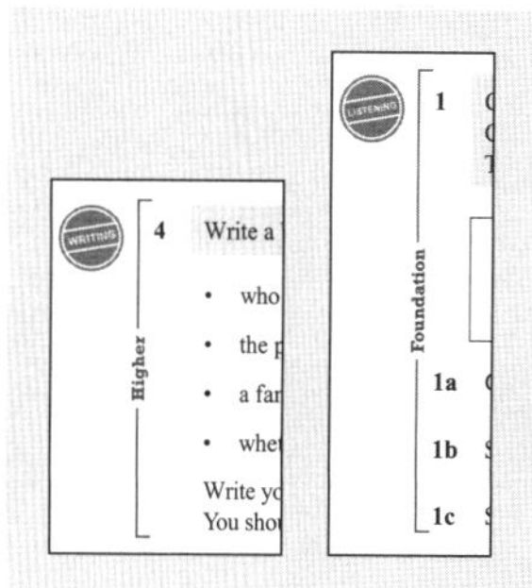

The CGP RevisionHub is full of resources

- You can use the online resources on the CGP RevisionHub **alongside this book** as you're revising.
- The RevisionHub contains all the **audio** you'll need for the **listening questions**, and **speaking tracks** so you can hear the teacher part for all the speaking questions in the book.
- There are printable versions of the **transcripts** and speaking and writing **mark schemes** as well.
- It's also got **worked answer videos** for some of the questions, so you can feel more confident about how to answer them.

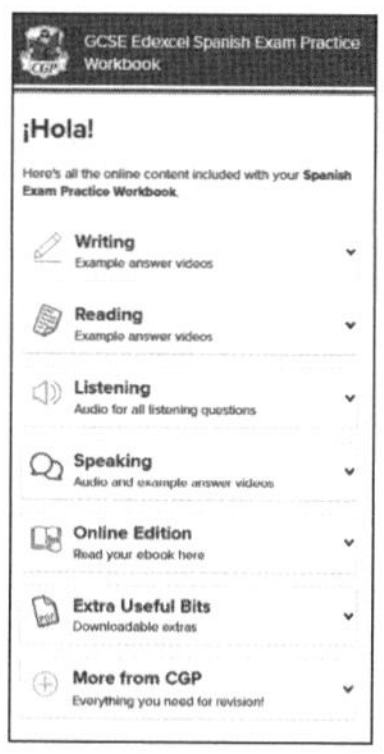

Revision Hub

Scan this QR code to access the CGP RevisionHub, or go to www.cgpbooks.co.uk/fiesta

How can you tell when an exam is upset?

It'll be in tiers. Ahem... anyway. It's well worth exploring the RevisionHub for this book. Not only because it's packed full of helpful videos, but also because you'll get to hear my beautiful voice. Lucky you.

Numbers, Times, Days and Dates

WRITING

1 Translate the following five sentences **into Spanish**.

Example Answer Video

1a I try to be active every day.

....

.... *[2 marks]*

1b Each morning, I walk for thirty minutes.

....

.... *[2 marks]*

Foundation

1c My girlfriend dances twice a week.

....

.... *[2 marks]*

1d In the summer, we prefer to ride our bicycles.

....

.... *[2 marks]*

1e Last year, I ran fifty kilometres in a competition.

....

.... *[2 marks]*

READING

2 Read Alba's article about her school. Answer the following questions **in English**. You do not need to write in full sentences.

Mi instituto es inmenso y la mayoría de las clases están en la primera planta. La clase de historia se sitúa en la segunda planta. El año pasado tuve dos horas de esa asignatura a la semana. Prefiero las clases que tienen pocos alumnos. Creo que menos gente es mejor porque es más fácil escuchar al profesor.

Higher

2a Where is the history classroom in Alba's school?

.... *[1 mark]*

2b Why does Alba like small classes?

.... *[1 mark]*

LISTENING

3 Lin is talking about birthdays. What does he say? Complete the gap in each sentence using a word or phrase from the box below. There are more words/phrases than gaps.

Listening Track 1

June	August	October	December
at night	in the morning		from midday
the cinema	his house	a restaurant	the park

3a Lin's cousin's birthday is in .... *[1 mark]*

3b He starts buying presents from .... *[1 mark]*

3c Lin's family usually celebrates .... *[1 mark]*

3d They like to have parties at .... *[1 mark]*

3e Lin would prefer to celebrate his birthday at .... *[1 mark]*

LISTENING

Higher

4a Listen to Sebastian talk about a failed trip to Madrid. What does he say? Listen to the recording and put a cross in each one of the **three** correct boxes.

Listening Track 2

	A His wife was ill.
	B He booked a morning flight.
	C There was little traffic on the main road.
	D His flight was delayed.
	E There were no train tickets left.
	F He has been sending letters.

[3 marks]

4b Sebastian now shares some information about his future travel plans. Listen to the recording and answer the questions **in English**. You do not need to write in full sentences.

i) How much money will Sebastian spend on his transport?

.... *[1 mark]*

ii) Why is he looking for a hotel near the airport?

.... *[1 mark]*

iii) What time will he arrive in Madrid?

.... *[1 mark]*

Score:

Questions and Being Polite

READING

Foundation

1 Read these messages sent to a restaurant.

Nadia: Organizo una fiesta sorpresa para una amiga. Entonces, ¿es posible reservar una mesa para seis personas esta noche?

Omar: Ceno en su restaurante mañana y le escribo sobre la carta. ¿Me puede decir cuántas opciones vegetarianas hay, por favor?

Hugo: ¿A qué hora cierra el restaurante este viernes? Quisiera cenar allí, pero no puedo venir hasta tarde.

Who says what? Choose the correct answers.
Put a cross in the correct column for each question.

	Who...	**Nadia**	**Omar**	**Hugo**
a)	...is looking for vegetarian food?			
b)	...wants to know about closing times?			
c)	...needs a table for tonight?			
d)	...asks about the menu?			
e)	...is organising a friend's party?			
f)	...can't get to the restaurant until late?			

[1 mark]
[1 mark]
[1 mark]
[1 mark]
[1 mark]
[1 mark]

WRITING

Foundation

2 Describe the photo. Write four short sentences **in Spanish**.

2a .... *[2 marks]*

2b .... *[2 marks]*

2c .... *[2 marks]*

2d .... *[2 marks]*

LISTENING

3 A librarian is talking to some students. What does she mention?
Listen to the recording and put a cross in each one of the **three** correct boxes.

Listening Track 3

	A study spaces
	B opening hours
	C returning books
	D book recommendations
	E locating books
	F refreshments

[3 marks]

READING

4 Read Raúl's email to his new employer. Answer the following questions **in English**. You do not need to write in full sentences.

> Buenos días Señora Brown. Soy Raúl López y desde el lunes que viene formaré parte de su equipo. Quisiera hacerle unas preguntas antes de empezar.
>
> Primero, ¿hay algo más que debería preparar? Ya he tomado una foto para mi tarjeta de identidad — ¿a quién podría mandarla? Además, quiero preguntarle si es necesario llevar traje en la oficina para que tenga tiempo suficiente para comprarme uno.
>
> Tengo mi propio coche y por eso no tengo que depender del transporte público para llegar al trabajo. Sin embargo, vivo bastante lejos de la oficina y me costará mucho viajar allí. ¿Me podría decir si mis compañeros comparten coches para ir a la oficina?
>
> Finalmente, ¿existen algunas actividades sociales en la compañía? Acabo de llegar a la zona y no conozco a nadie aquí. Por lo tanto, querría conocer bien a mis compañeros. Un club de tenis sería perfecto porque los deportes me interesan muchísimo.

Higher

4a Why is Raúl writing to Mrs Brown?

.... *[1 mark]*

4b What has Raúl already prepared for the job?

.... *[1 mark]*

4c What does Raúl want to know about the dress code?

.... *[1 mark]*

4d What does Raúl ask about transport?

.... *[1 mark]*

4e Why does Raúl ask about social activities? (1 detail)

.... *[1 mark]*

Score:

Opinions

SPEAKING

Foundation

1 Your Mexican friend writes about his favourite hobby. Read out the text below to your teacher.

Speaking Track 1

Scan the QR code to hear the teacher part of the question, or you can find the transcript in the back of the book.

Me encanta ir al cine.
Siempre es una experiencia divertida.
Pero a veces prefiero ver las películas en casa.
Invito a mis amigos y pasamos toda la tarde juntos.
La próxima vez, me gustaría ver una película de terror.

- Once you have read the text, you will then be asked two questions related to what you have read.
- You are expected to say a few words or a short phrase/sentence in response to each question. One-word answers will not be sufficient to gain full marks.

[12 marks]

LISTENING

Foundation

2 Sofía is visiting Seville and she wants to know more about the city. What does she find out? Listen to the recording and complete the following tables **in English**. You do not need to write in full sentences.

Listening Track 4

2a

Reason to visit the palace
....

[1 mark]

2b

What to see in the evenings
....

[1 mark]

2c

Quality of the food
....

[1 mark]

LISTENING

3 Luisa is giving her opinion on various foods and drinks. What does she say? Complete the gap in each sentence using a word from the box below. There are more words than gaps.

Listening Track 5

milk	water	coffee	tea
meat	fish	cake	chocolate

3a With breakfast, Luisa has .... *[1 mark]*

3b Every day she drinks .... *[1 mark]*

3c Luisa can't eat .... *[1 mark]*

3d She wants to eat less .... *[1 mark]*

READING

Higher

4 Read Indra's blog post about her interest in writing.

Me encanta escribir historias. Creo mundos interesantes en mi mente y luego escribo sobre los personajes que viven en estos lugares. Sería maravilloso publicar una novela en el futuro.
También disfruto escribiendo canciones para cantarlas en una banda con mis amigos. El próximo mes, participaremos en un gran espectáculo y estoy nerviosa. Sin embargo, pienso que será una experiencia emocionante que nunca olvidaré.

What does Indra say about writing?
Complete the tables **in English**. You do not need to write in full sentences.

4a

What she writes stories about (1 detail)
....

[1 mark]

4b

Her future writing goal
....

[1 mark]

4c

Why she writes songs (1 detail)
....

[1 mark]

4d

Her feelings about the show (1 detail)
....

[1 mark]

Score:

About Yourself and My Family & Friends

READING

Foundation

1 Translate the following sentences **into English**.

Example Answer Video

1a Paso mucho tiempo con mi familia.

.... *[2 marks]*

1b Me llevo muy bien con mi hermana.

.... *[2 marks]*

1c Se llama Luisa y tiene los ojos verdes.

.... *[2 marks]*

1d El domingo pasado fuimos a un museo juntos.

.... *[2 marks]*

1e Hoy visitamos a nuestro primo en la costa por su cumpleaños.

.... *[2 marks]*

LISTENING

2 Elena and Malek are talking about their families.
What do they say? Listen to the recording and complete the sentences by putting a cross in the correct box for each question.

Listening Track 6

2a Elena's mum is...

	A moving house.
	B getting married.
	C having a baby.

[1 mark]

2b Malek's grandfather...

	A needs his wheelchair more.
	B helps around the house.
	C lives in a flat nearby.

[1 mark]

2c Malek's aunt...

	A currently works abroad.
	B is moving in.
	C lives by the hospital.

[1 mark]

LISTENING

Listening Track 7

3 You are going to hear someone talking about their family.

Sentences 1 and 2: Write down the missing words in the gaps provided. In each gap, you will write one word **in Spanish**.

Sentences 3, 4, 5 and 6: Write down the full sentences that you hear in the spaces provided, **in Spanish**.

Higher

3a Sentence 1

Mi .... está .... *[2 marks]*

3b Sentence 2

Estoy .... de .... a mi .... *[2 marks]*

3c Sentence 3

....

.... *[2 marks]*

3d Sentence 4

....

.... *[2 marks]*

3e Sentence 5

....

.... *[2 marks]*

3f Sentence 6

....

.... *[2 marks]*

WRITING

Foundation

4 Write an article about your family and friends. You **must** include the following points:

- a description of your family
- your opinion of pets
- when you will next see your friends.

Write your answer **in Spanish**. You should aim to write between 40 and 50 words. *[14 marks]*

Score:

Describing People and Relationships

LISTENING

Foundation

1 Omar is describing what he looks like. What does he mention?
Listen to the recording and put a cross in each one of the **three** correct boxes.

Listening Track 8

	A Black hair
	B Long hair
	C Glasses
	D Blue eyes
	E Brown hair
	F Short (height)

[3 marks]

WRITING

2 Write to your friend about your relationships. You **must** include the following points:

- your relationship with your family
- your opinion of having children with reasons
- what you did to help a friend recently
- what qualities you would like your future partner to have.

Write your answer **in Spanish**. You should aim to write between 80 and 90 words. *[18 marks]*

SPEAKING

Higher

3 Leya has contributed to a blog about her family relationships.
Read out the text below to your teacher.

Speaking Track 2

Me llevo muy bien con mis padres porque son simpáticos.

Ayer discutí con mi hermano, pero normalmente me hace reír un montón.

Mucha gente dice que mi abuela y yo nos parecemos, lo que me gusta mucho.

Tiene la sonrisa más preciosa y espero ser tan feliz como ella cuando tenga su edad.

- Once you have read the text, you will then be asked two questions related to what you have read.
- You are expected to say a few words or a short phrase/sentence in response to each question. One-word answers will not be sufficient to gain full marks.

[12 marks]

READING

4 Read Monika's description of her friend Jalil.

Conocí a Jalil en mi clase de inglés. Le reconocí porque tenía el pelo verde y las gafas rojas. Como yo tenía el pelo rosa, me dijo que le gustaba mi estilo y comenzó a hablarme.*

Después, tomamos el almuerzo juntos y somos amigos desde entonces. Soy más trabajadora que Jalil pero él es más alegre. Disfrutamos haciendo deportes juntos, pero tenemos gustos musicales diferentes. Encontramos divertidas las mismas cosas. Por ejemplo se ríe de los mismos programas divertidos que yo.

**reconocí = I noticed*

Complete the gap in each sentence using a word or phrase from the box below.
There are more words/phrases than gaps.

green	pink	red	
food	comedies	subjects	music

4a Monika noticed Jalil because he had .... hair. *[1 mark]*

4b Jalil and Monika like different .... *[1 mark]*

4c However, they enjoy the same .... *[1 mark]*

READING

Higher

5 Translate the following paragraph **into English**.

Cuando era pequeña, era la más baja en mi clase. Ya no soy baja, sino alta. También tengo el pelo largo y moreno que llevo en un pañuelo. Varias figuras artísticas han tenido una influencia inmensa sobre mi estilo. El arte y la moda siempre me han ayudado a expresarme sin miedo.

....

....

....

....

....

....

.... *[10 marks]*

Score:

Role Models and Celebrations

WRITING

Foundation

1 Describe the photo. Write four short sentences **in Spanish**.

1a .... *[2 marks]*

1b .... *[2 marks]*

1c .... *[2 marks]*

1d .... *[2 marks]*

LISTENING

2 Andrea, Javier and Luis are talking about celebrations. What do they say?
Listen to the recording and complete the following tables **in English**.
You do not need to write in full sentences.

Listening Track 9

2a

	When her parents have a party
Andrea	....

[1 mark]

2b

	Reason he wants to celebrate
Javier	....

[1 mark]

2c

	Why he can't have a party
Luis	....

[1 mark]

LISTENING

Listening Track 10

Higher

3 Julia is talking about her birthday party. What does she say? Listen to the recording and complete the sentences by putting a cross in the correct box for each question.

3a Julia's birthday is...

	A	four weeks after the party.
	B	four days before the party.
	C	on the 4th July.

[1 mark]

3b She wants the party to be...

	A	smaller than last year's.
	B	bigger than last year's.
	C	expensive and fashionable.

[1 mark]

3c Julia is anxious that...

	A	her boyfriend can't attend the party.
	B	there will be too many people again.
	C	her family won't be able to come.

[1 mark]

3d She hopes that...

	A	she can find a beautiful cake.
	B	her boyfriend has ordered a cake.
	C	the cake she has ordered arrives on time.

[1 mark]

WRITING

Higher

4 Write a blog post about role models. You **must** include the following points:

- who you respect and relate to
- the pros and cons of being a role model
- a famous person or group that you liked in the past
- whether you want to be famous in the future.

Write your answer **in Spanish**.
You should aim to write between 130 and 150 words.

[22 marks]

Score:

Food

WRITING

Foundation

1 Describe the photo. Write four short sentences **in Spanish**.

1a .... *[2 marks]*

1b .... *[2 marks]*

1c .... *[2 marks]*

1d .... *[2 marks]*

LISTENING

Higher

2 Rosalía is talking about healthy eating. What does she say? Listen to the recording and complete the sentences by putting a cross in the correct box for each question.

Listening Track 11

2a When her daughter stopped eating breakfast, Rosalía...

	A discussed it with her partner.
	B felt concerned for her.
	C did some research alone.

[1 mark]

2b Scientists say that breakfast is...

	A beneficial.
	B unnecessary.
	C optional.

[1 mark]

2c Rosalía recommends that people...

	A only eat fruit for breakfast.
	B eat a balanced breakfast.
	C avoid eggs at breakfast.

[1 mark]

READING

3 Read Nadim's blog post on his meal at a restaurant.

> *El sábado pasado fui a un restaurante mexicano y fue excelente. Comí mucha comida tradicional, como tortillas con carne y arroz. Después, quería pedir los churros de estilo mexicano, pero no había ninguno. Entonces, al final no tomé postre porque no quería otra opción.*
>
> *Siempre me gusta terminar la cena con una bebida caliente. Normalmente prefiero el té, pero esta vez escogí el café. Era fuerte y riquísimo. Voy a comprar más café mexicano en el futuro.*

Complete the gap in each sentence using a word from the box below. There are more words than gaps.

meat		vegetables	eggs
starter	coffee	tea	dessert

3a Nadim ate traditional corn pancakes with .... *[1 mark]*

3b He didn't like the other .... options. *[1 mark]*

3c Nadim really enjoyed the .... *[1 mark]*

LISTENING

Foundation

4 Sasha is talking about his diet.
What is mentioned?
Listen to the recording and put a cross in each one of the **three** correct boxes.

Listening Track 12

	A cold drinks
	B desserts
	C lunch
	D dinner
	E vegan food
	F vegetables

[3 marks]

Score:

Physical & Mental Wellbeing and Illnesses & Treatments

SPEAKING

1 You are at a doctor's surgery in Spain, and you are talking to the doctor. Listen to the recording to hear the part of the teacher. They will speak first.

Speaking Track 3

- Your teacher will ask questions **in Spanish** and you must answer **in Spanish**.
- You are expected to say a few words or a short phrase / sentence in response to each prompt. One-word answers will not be sufficient to gain full marks.

Task:

1. Say why you are there to see the doctor.
2. Say what kind of exercise you do to be fit.
3. Say whether you think you have a healthy diet.
4. Tell the doctor about another health problem you have.
5. Ask a question about where you can get medicine.

[10 marks]

READING

Higher

2 Read this post on an online health forum. Vicente is talking about mental wellbeing.

Muchos jóvenes sufren de problemas de salud mental y deberíamos apoyarles más. Por ejemplo podemos animarles a llamar a las líneas de ayuda.

Hay otras cosas que todo el mundo puede hacer para ayudarse. Para mí, dormir lo suficiente es crucial para cuidar de la mente. Por lo tanto, tendré que acostarme mucho más temprano y no comer justo antes de ir a la cama.

Mis amigos y yo pasábamos demasiado tiempo en el móvil y era negativo para mí. Por lo tanto, ahora utilizo menos los dispositivos.

Put a cross in each one of the **three** correct boxes.

Vicente says that...

	A everyone is worrying more.
	B young people need greater support.
	C he needs to eat more healthily.
	D he wants to change his sleep routine.
	E he's trying to reduce his screen time.
	F he spends a lot of time chatting to friends.

[3 marks]

LISTENING

3 Karima is talking about her health issues. What does she say? Listen to the recording and complete the sentences by putting a cross in the correct box for each question.

Listening Track 13

Foundation

3a Karima says that her shoulder...

	A is burnt.
	B hurts.
	C is broken.

[1 mark]

3b To help her problem, she often...

	A visits a doctor.
	B has a hot bath.
	C takes medicine.

[1 mark]

3c She is also trying to...

	A exercise more.
	B relax more.
	C sleep more.

[1 mark]

3d Unfortunately, she can't...

	A practise certain sports.
	B play instruments.
	C paint her room.

[1 mark]

WRITING

4 Write a letter to your friend about healthy habits. You **must** include the following points:

Foundation Answer Video

Higher Answer Video

- what you do to take care of your mental health
- your opinion of taking drugs with reasons
- what you have done recently to be healthy
- a type of exercise you would like to do in the future.

Write your answer **in Spanish**. You should aim to write between 80 and 90 words. *[18 marks]*

Score:

Music, Cinema and TV

LISTENING

Foundation

1 Carla is talking about the music she likes to listen to. What does she say?
Complete the gap in each sentence using a word or phrase from the box below.
There are more words/phrases than gaps.

Listening Track 14

cycling	walking	in class	at work
pop	classical	rock	

1a Carla likes listening to music when she's .... *[1 mark]*

1b She isn't allowed to listen to music while .... *[1 mark]*

1c She prefers listening to .... music when studying. *[1 mark]*

LISTENING

2 An advert for a new cinema is on the radio. What does it mention?
Listen to the recording and put a cross in each one of the **three** correct boxes.

Listening Track 15

	A the picture quality
	B the special effects
	C the drinks
	D the food
	E the opening times
	F the ticket price

[3 marks]

WRITING

Higher

3 Translate the following paragraph **into Spanish**.

I love watching TV because it is very relaxing. I used to watch nature documentaries after school but now I prefer to watch the news or a series. For me, films are quite difficult to watch. They last much longer than TV programmes. I will start watching the new season of my current favourite drama tonight.

....

....

....

....

....

.... *[10 marks]*

READING

4a Read Diego's blog post about a new TV show.

> *Mi programa favorito vuelve a nuestras televisiones en tres semanas. Estuve triste cuando terminó hace ocho años, pero una serie especial viene en julio.*
>
> *Cuando lo veía de niño, diez personas normales cantaban para ganar dinero. En el nuevo, los cantantes son famosos y escogen una organización. Si ganan, su organización recibirá dinero. El director quiere hacer sonreír al público con el programa y también ayudar a la gente en dificultad.*
>
> *Las revistas están llenas de ideas y* ***suposiciones*** *sobre quién participará, pero la verdad es todavía un secreto.*

Complete the sentences below. Put a cross in the correct box for each question.

i) Diego's favourite show finished...

	A three weeks ago.
	B eight years ago.
	C in July.

[1 mark]

ii) In the old show, contestants were...

	A children.
	B celebrities.
	C regular people.

[1 mark]

iii) In the new version, the singers...

	A are not famous.
	B choose a charity to help.
	C win a record deal.

[1 mark]

iv) The director wants to...

	A help those in need.
	B be famous.
	C get rich.

[1 mark]

4b Which of these is the best translation of the word ***suposiciones***?

Put a cross in the correct box.

	A guesses
	B plans
	C profiles

[1 mark]

Score:

Sports, Going Out and Other Hobbies

READING

Foundation

1 Read these messages in a group chat about hobbies.

> **Ana:** Cuando voy al teatro, siempre como en un restaurante italiano después. Me gusta cocinar en casa también.
> **Lin:** Tengo pasión por el arte. El dibujo es divertido y me gusta pintar. El baile también es hermoso practicarlo.
> **Cris:** Escribir me importa mucho. De momento escribo para mi blog cada semana pero quiero escribir ficción pronto.

Who says what? Choose the correct answers.
Put a cross in the correct column for each question.

	Who...	Ana	Lin	Cris
a)	...wants to write fiction?			
b)	...enjoys drawing?			
c)	...has a blog?			
d)	...goes out for food?			
e)	...likes dancing?			
f)	...enjoys cooking?			

[1 mark]
[1 mark]
[1 mark]
[1 mark]
[1 mark]
[1 mark]

LISTENING

2 Alejandro is talking about reading. What does he say? Listen to the recording and complete the sentences by putting a cross in the correct box for each question.

Listening Track 16

2a Alejandro prefers to read...

	A fiction.
	B non-fiction.
	C news stories.

[1 mark]

2b Reading has helped him...

	A be healthier.
	B find studying easier.
	C make friends.

[1 mark]

2c He has learnt that reading can help people to...

	A sleep.
	B communicate.
	C understand each other.

[1 mark]

SPEAKING

Foundation

3 You are at a leisure centre in Madrid and you are talking to an employee. Listen to the recording to hear the part of the teacher. They will speak first.

Speaking Track 4

- Your teacher will ask questions **in Spanish** and you must answer **in Spanish**.
- You are expected to say a few words or a short phrase / sentence in response to each prompt. One-word answers will not be sufficient to gain full marks.

Task:

1. Say why you are at the leisure centre.
2. Say what days you want to go.
3. Give your opinion about sports.
4. Say what sport you want to try.
5. Ask a question about the classes they offer.

[10 marks]

READING

Higher

4 Translate the following paragraph **into English**.

Example Answer Video

Hago deportes desde hace nueve años. La natación es mi pasión y suelo practicarla tres veces a la semana. La temporada pasada mi amigo y yo participamos en una competición y él ganó un premio. Cuando haga mis exámenes tendré menos tiempo para hacer deporte. Sin embargo, después de terminarlos volveré a las competiciones.

....

....

....

....

.... *[10 marks]*

WRITING

Higher

5 Write a blog post about free time. You **must** include the following points:

- where you like to go out with friends
- the pros and cons of eating in restaurants
- a hobby that you liked when you were younger
- an activity you would like to try in the future.

Write your answer **in Spanish**.
You should aim to write between 130 and 150 words. *[22 marks]*

Score:

Mixed Practice — Foundation

READING

Foundation

1a Read your pen-pal Miguel's introductory email to you.

> Vivo en el sur de Argentina. Tengo una familia grande y todos somos argentinos. Pronto vamos a la casa de mi abuela para su fiesta de cumpleaños. Le compramos muchos regalos. Quiero darle unos ***guantes*** nuevos porque le encanta la ropa y siempre busca proteger sus manos.

Complete the sentences below. Put a cross in the correct box for each question.

i) Miguel's family...

	A lives in the north.
	B is small.
	C is Argentinian.

[1 mark]

ii) Miguel's grandmother...

	A lives in Miguel's house.
	B is having a birthday party.
	C buys a lot of gifts.

[1 mark]

1b Which of these is the best translation of the word ***guantes***?

Put a cross in the correct box.

	A rings
	B boots
	C gloves

[1 mark]

WRITING

Foundation

2 Write an article about a restaurant you like.
You **must** include the following points:

- a description of the restaurant
- your opinion of their menu
- when you will next visit the restaurant.

Write your answer **in Spanish**. You should aim to write between 40 and 50 words. *[14 marks]*

WRITING

Foundation

3 Describe the photo.
Write four short sentences **in Spanish**.

Example Answer Video

3a .... *[2 marks]*

3b .... *[2 marks]*

3c .... *[2 marks]*

3d .... *[2 marks]*

READING

Foundation

4 Read Diego's email.

> *Estoy jugando a un buen juego en la videoconsola y quiero terminarlo hoy. Me gusta jugar a videojuegos pero mi pasatiempo favorito es pintar. Es la única actividad que hago todos los días. Normalmente pinto cuadros pequeños pero ahora estoy haciendo uno más grande para mis padres.*

Put a cross in each one of the **three** correct boxes.

Diego...

	A is playing on his laptop.
	B has a game he wants to finish.
	C paints every day.
	D likes gaming the most.
	E paints with his parents.
	F usually creates small paintings.

[3 marks]

LISTENING

5 You are going to hear someone talking about their free-time activities.

Listening Track 17

Sentence 1: Write down the missing words in the gaps provided.
In each gap, you will write one word **in Spanish**.

Sentence 2: Write down the full sentence that you hear in the space provided, **in Spanish**.

Foundation

5a Sentence 1

Me encanta .... las .... *[2 marks]*

5b Sentence 2

....

.... *[2 marks]*

READING

6 Translate the following sentences **into English**.

6a Esta mañana, necesito ir al hospital.

....

.... *[2 marks]*

6b Tengo una cita porque me duele la garganta.

....

.... *[2 marks]*

Foundation

6c Ya tomo tabletas y son bastante fuertes.

....

.... *[2 marks]*

6d Los doctores son simpáticos y me ayudan mucho.

....

.... *[2 marks]*

6e La semana pasada, mi hermana también estuvo muy enferma.

....

.... *[2 marks]*

READING

Foundation

7 Read this extract from Karima's diary.

Por la mañana tuve una clase de natación pero antes fui al supermercado. Ahora voy al cine a ver dos películas con mis amigos y cada una dura sólo una hora y media. No vamos a salir del cine hasta las seis. Después, llevaré a mi hermano a un concierto para ver a su grupo favorito. Desafortunadamente, tenemos que volver temprano porque mañana necesito visitar al doctor.

Put a cross in each one of the **three** correct boxes.

Karima...

	A went to the supermarket first.
	B had a painting class.
	C is going to the cinema alone.
	D will leave the cinema in the evening.
	E will see her favourite band tonight.
	F has a medical appointment tomorrow.

[3 marks]

SPEAKING

Foundation

8 Choose **one** of the pictures below to describe.
Make notes on it to use during the test.

Speaking Track 5

Your teacher will ask you to describe the picture. You should talk for approximately **one and a half to two minutes**. Your description must cover the **people, location and activity** shown in the picture.

After you have spoken about the content of the picture, your teacher will ask you two questions about your chosen picture. Then, they will ask you some questions related to any of the topics within the theme of **My Personal World**.

Picture 1

Picture 2

[28 marks]

Score:

Mixed Practice — Both Tiers

READING

1 Read Omar's blog post about the seasons.

Example Answer Video

> Prefiero viajar a climas tropicales cuando hace frío en el invierno. En el verano, mi padre y yo jugamos al baloncesto todos los domingos. Mi estación favorita es el otoño porque me gusta caminar debajo de los árboles bonitos. Me divierto mucho en el jardín en primavera también.

Complete the sentences below. Put a cross in the correct box for each question.

1a In the summer, Omar and his father play...

	A basketball.
	B football.
	C computer games.

[1 mark]

1b In which of the following seasons does Omar **not** mention spending time outside?

	A autumn
	B winter
	C spring

[1 mark]

1c Why is autumn Omar's favourite season?

	A He likes walking under the trees.
	B He likes it when the weather gets cold.
	C He enjoys spending time in the garden.

[1 mark]

LISTENING

2 Sasha and Jalil are talking about health problems. What do they say? Listen to the recording and complete the following tables **in English**. You do not need to write in full sentences.

Listening Track 18

2a

	Where she has to exercise
Sasha	....

[1 mark]

2b

	Body part he takes medicine for
Jalil	....

[1 mark]

WRITING

3 Write to your friend about music.
You **must** include the following points:

- your favourite musical artist
- your opinion of pop music with reasons
- the type of music you last listened to
- a concert you will go to in the future.

Write your answer **in Spanish**. You should aim to write between 80 and 90 words. *[18 marks]*

LISTENING

4 Carla is talking about her family. What does she say?
Complete the gap in each sentence using a word or phrase from the box below.
There are more words/phrases than gaps.

Listening Track 19

mother	stepbrother	sister	stepfather
neighbourhood	house	city	
loud	funny	strict	hard-working

4a Carla doesn't talk much to her .... *[1 mark]*

4b She gets on very well with her .... *[1 mark]*

4c Carla and her aunt live in the same .... *[1 mark]*

4d Her aunt is .... *[1 mark]*

4e Her mother is very .... *[1 mark]*

WRITING

5 Write to your friend about food.
You **must** include the following points:

- what you like to eat at home
- your opinion of one type of food with reasons
- the last time you went out to eat
- what you will eat next weekend.

Write your answer **in Spanish**. You should aim to write between 80 and 90 words. *[18 marks]*

Score:

Mixed Practice — Higher

SPEAKING

Higher

1 David, your friend, writes about his daily routine.
Read out the text below to your teacher.

Speaking Track 6

Example Answer Video

> Trato de tener una rutina tranquila por la mañana.
>
> Sin embargo, hay mucho ruido en casa ya que tengo hermanos menores.
>
> Prefiero terminar mis deberes antes de la cena, pero no siempre es posible porque tengo tareas.
>
> A pesar de todo, diría que disfruto viviendo con mi familia y pasamos la mayoría de nuestro tiempo juntos.

- Once you have read the text, you will then be asked two questions related to what you have read.
- You are expected to say a few words or a short phrase/sentence in response to each question. One-word answers will not be sufficient to gain full marks.

[12 marks]

READING

Higher

2 Read this news article about unhealthy lifestyles.

> *Un estudio reciente ha reconocido que hay una falta de ejercicio entre muchos ciudadanos. Tampoco tienen una dieta equilibrada a causa del poco conocimiento que tienen sobre la comida sana.*
>
> *Los científicos esperan discutir los resultados del estudio con el gobierno. Quieren que el gobierno haga algo para informar a la gente afectada. Por lo tanto, a través de unas campañas sociales quieren crear* ***conciencia*** *entre el público sobre cómo cambiar las malas costumbres y comer mejor.*

2a Answer the following questions in English. You do not need to write in full sentences.

i) What problems has a recent study revealed? (1 detail)

.... *[1 mark]*

ii) Who do the scientists want to help them with the results of the study?

.... *[1 mark]*

2b Which of these is the best translation of the word ***conciencia***?

	A unrest
	B awareness
	C support

[1 mark]

LISTENING

Listening Track 20

Higher

3a Listen to Diego's podcast about an accident he had. What does he say?
Listen to the recording and put a cross in each one of the **three** correct boxes.

	A A car hit Diego.
	B His left leg is broken.
	C He has to use a wheelchair.
	D He can't leave his bed much.
	E The doctor says he can't exercise.
	F In two weeks, he has an appointment.

[3 marks]

3b Diego now shares more information about his recovery. Listen to the recording, then answer the questions **in English**. You do not need to write in full sentences.

i) Why didn't Diego like the magazine his grandma bought him?

.... *[1 mark]*

ii) What did Diego's band do to cheer him up?

.... *[1 mark]*

iii) Why has the doctor recommended swimming?

.... *[1 mark]*

iv) What is Diego looking forward to?

.... *[1 mark]*

WRITING

Higher

4 Translate the following paragraph **into Spanish**.

> I have just organised a party for the 12th December. It starts at quarter to seven and it is going to last for four hours. Thirty-eight people will attend the event, including my whole family. I went to another celebration recently and it was very boring. However, I really liked the food.

....

....

....

....

.... *[10 marks]*

SPEAKING

Higher

5 Choose **one** of the pictures below to describe.
Make notes on it to use during the test.

Speaking Track 7

Your teacher will ask you to describe the picture. You should talk for approximately **one and a half to two minutes**. Your description must cover the **people, location and activity** shown in the picture.

After you have spoken about the content of the picture, your teacher will ask you two questions about your chosen picture. Then, they will ask you some questions related to any of the topics within the theme of **My Neighbourhood**.

Picture 1

Picture 2

[28 marks]

READING

Higher

6 Translate the following paragraph **into English**.

Mi pasión es la cocina ya que es una parte importante de la cultura mexicana. Mi madre odia la comida basura, entonces siempre prepara platos frescos. Además, nos enseñó a mis hermanos y a mí a cocinar cuando éramos pequeños. Yo era vegano, pero ya no porque era difícil seguir esa dieta. Me encantaría abrir un restaurante vegetariano.

....

....

....

....

.... *[10 marks]*

READING

7 Read Karima's article about her relationship with her twin.

Tener una hermana gemela es especial. Mi hermana Lola y yo nos parecemos mucho porque ambas somos pelirrojas y tenemos los ojos verdes. No obstante, hay algunas diferencias entre nosotras. Ella es un poco más alta y tiene el pelo más oscuro. Sin embargo, nuestras personalidades son lo más distinto entre nosotras.

Por ejemplo, yo soy nerviosa cuando estoy en grupos grandes pero ella siempre ha sido más cómoda en ellos. Además, a ella le gusta bailar con sus amigos. Cantamos juntas en una banda, pero normalmente prefiero hacer actividades sola como pintar.

Sin embargo, me encanta tener a Lola siempre que quiero compañía. Es lo mejor de tener una hermana gemela. El año pasado tuve dificultades con mi salud mental y Lola me ayudó muchísimo. Fue la primera persona que me hizo reír cuando estaba triste. Nos entendemos a la perfección.

Mucha gente siempre nos quiere comparar — por ejemplo quién es más lista o más guapa. Esto no nos importa, pero puede resultar irritante.*

**resultar = be*

Answer the following questions **in English**.
You do not need to write in full sentences.

Higher

7a How does Karima look different to Lola? (1 detail)

....

7b According to Karima, what is the main difference between her and Lola?

....

7c What interest do Karima and Lola share?

....

7d What is Karima's favourite aspect of being a twin?

....

7e What can be difficult about being a twin?

....

Score:

Where You Live and At Home

WRITING

Foundation

1 Describe the photo.
Write four short sentences **in Spanish**.

1a .... *[2 marks]*

1b .... *[2 marks]*

1c .... *[2 marks]*

1d .... *[2 marks]*

LISTENING

2 Nadia is telling you about where she lives. What does she say?
Listen to the recording and complete the sentences by putting a cross in the correct box for each question.

Listening Track 21

2a Nadia's house is located...

	A in the countryside.
	B in the city centre.
	C on the corner of a main road.

[1 mark]

2b Nadia would like to live...

	A somewhere with more space.
	B in a more modern house.
	C in her own flat.

[1 mark]

2c Her parents...

	A don't like their neighbourhood.
	B like the city centre.
	C are looking to move house.

[1 mark]

READING

Foundation

3 Read these comments from Jalil and Sasha. Complete the following tables **in English**. You do not need to write in full sentences.

Example Answer Video

Jalil : Me levanto a las siete y primero me visto. Cada tarde es mi responsabilidad limpiar la cocina, y después veo la tele en mi habitación. Pero no me duermo hasta las diez y cuarto.

3a

One detail about his mornings	....
When he goes to bed	....

[1 mark]

[1 mark]

Sasha : Mis hermanos y yo ayudamos en casa. Siempre disfruto preparando la cena, pero creo que lavar la ropa es aburrido. Esta semana voy a terminar mis deberes temprano porque el sábado voy de viaje con mi familia.

3b

One thing she likes doing to help	....
What she will do at the weekend	....

[1 mark]

[1 mark]

SPEAKING

Higher

4 Mario, your Colombian friend, writes about his views on where he lives. Read out the text below to your teacher.

Speaking Track 8

Soy habitante de un barrio urbano en Medellín.

Se sitúa en las afueras de la ciudad y es muy hermoso.

Existen sitios guay para reunirse con amigos, como parques, tiendas e incluso varios gimnasios.

Para mí lo mejor de vivir aquí es la comunidad, ya que nunca me faltan personas que me apoyan.

Scan the QR code to hear the teacher part of the question, or you can find the transcript in the back of the book.

- Once you have read the text, you will then be asked two questions related to what you have read.
- You are expected to say a few words or a short phrase/sentence in response to each question. One-word answers will not be sufficient to gain full marks.

[12 marks]

Score:

The Local Area

LISTENING

1 You are going to hear someone talking about their local area.

Listening Track 22

Sentences 1, 2 and 3: Write down the missing words in the gaps provided. In each gap, you will write one word **in Spanish**.

Sentences 4 and 5: Write down the full sentences that you hear in the spaces provided, **in Spanish**.

Foundation

1a Sentence 1

Mi .... tiene .... bares. *[2 marks]*

1b Sentence 2

Me gusta .... el .... *[2 marks]*

1c Sentence 3

La .... principal es .... *[2 marks]*

1d Sentence 4

....

.... *[2 marks]*

1e Sentence 5

....

.... *[2 marks]*

WRITING

Higher

2 Write a blog about your local area.
You **must** include the following points:

- what you like about your neighbourhood
- the pros and cons of living in a city
- the last place you visited in your local area
- what you will do in your local area this weekend.

Write your answer **in Spanish**.
You should aim to write between 130 and 150 words. *[22 marks]*

LISTENING

3 Paula, Malek and Daniel are talking about where they live. What do they say? Listen to the recording and complete the sentences by putting a cross in the correct box for each question.

Listening Track 23

3a Paula thinks her area lacks...

	A shops.
	B green spaces.
	C clean streets.

[1 mark]

3b Malek says the cinema is...

	A in the city centre.
	B next to a café.
	C in the south of the city.

[1 mark]

3c Daniel...

	A lives in a busy area.
	B will shop at the supermarket.
	C likes supporting small businesses.

[1 mark]

READING

Higher

4 Read this magazine article about a Spanish town.

Durante el verano, vimos cambios positivos en nuestra zona local. El gimnasio introdujo muchas actividades nuevas. Además, un teatro abrió sus puertas al público después de estar cerrado por seis meses. En la página siguiente se puede obtener un descuento para un espectáculo del próximo mes. Finalmente, hay otra historia emocionante. Pronto habrá una nueva **peluquería** en la plaza. Será un lugar popular con todo el mundo porque ofrecerá varios estilos de cabello hermosos.

4a Answer the following questions **in English**.
You do not need to write in full sentences.

i) What has changed in the local area over the summer? (1 detail)

.... *[1 mark]*

ii) What is the magazine currently offering to readers?

.... *[1 mark]*

4b Which of these is the best translation of the word ***peluquería***?
Put a cross in the correct box.

	A a shoe shop
	B a hairdresser's
	C a jeweller's

[1 mark]

Score:

Shopping, Directions and Weather

SPEAKING

Foundation

1 You are in a tourist information centre in a Spanish town. Listen to the recording to hear the part of the teacher. They will speak first.

Speaking Track 9

- Your teacher will ask questions **in Spanish** and you must answer **in Spanish**.
- You are expected to say a few words or a short phrase / sentence in response to each prompt. One-word answers will not be sufficient to gain full marks.

Example Answer Video

Task:

1. Say what you want to do in the town.
2. Say where your hotel is located.
3. Say what weather you prefer.
4. Give your opinion about the town.
5. Ask a question about places to eat in the town.

[10 marks]

WRITING

Higher

2 Translate the following paragraph **into Spanish**.

Today is sunny and warm. Last week, it was windy and it rained for three days. The worst thing was that I couldn't go to the park with my friends. However, according to the news, there will be no more rain this week. Therefore, I will be able to spend lots of time outdoors.

....

....

....

....

....

.... *[10 marks]*

WRITING

3 Write an email to your friend about shopping.
You **must** include the following points:

- what the shops in your area are like
- your opinion of online shopping with reasons
- the last time you went shopping
- what you will buy the next time you go shopping.

Write your answer **in Spanish**. You should aim to write between 80 and 90 words. *[18 marks]*

READING

4 Read this advertisement about a sports centre in a Spanish city.

Recientemente abrió la sala de baile en nuestro centro deportivo. Está delante del gimnasio y a la izquierda de la tienda. En nuestra tienda se puede comprar ropa deportiva como chaquetas y calcetines. Las zapatillas de deporte son increíblemente populares. Nuestra piscina es muy grande y se encuentra detrás del centro. Cerró el mes pasado porque había mucha nieve.

4a Complete the sentences below. Put a cross in the correct box for each question.

i) You can find the dance hall...

	A behind the pool.
	B to the right of the gym.
	C to the left of the shop.

[1 mark]

ii) The shop's best-sellers are...

	A jackets.
	B trainers.
	C socks.

[1 mark]

4b Answer the following questions **in English**.
You do not need to write in full sentences.

i) Where is the swimming pool?

.... *[1 mark]*

ii) Why was the pool closed recently?

.... *[1 mark]*

Score:

Environmental Problems, Effects and Protection

READING

1 Translate the following sentences **into English**.

Foundation

1a Me gusta montar en bicicleta.

.... *[2 marks]*

1b Es mejor para el medio ambiente que viajar en coche.

.... *[2 marks]*

1c Ayer cogí el autobús para ir al colegio y fue muy rápido.

.... *[2 marks]*

1d El transporte público protege el planeta, ya que usa menos energía.

.... *[2 marks]*

LISTENING

2 Cris is talking about environmental problems. What does he say?
Complete the gap in each sentence using a word or phrase from the box below.
There are more words/phrases than gaps.

Listening Track 24

cloud	sun	wind	snow
mountains	green spaces	seas	forests

F

2a Cris says that in Spain there is more .... than before. *[1 mark]*

2b Some areas receive a lot of .... *[1 mark]*

2c He says we need to do more to protect our .... *[1 mark]*

2d Cris likes to help by cleaning .... *[1 mark]*

WRITING

3 Write a letter to your friend about the environment.
You **must** include the following points:

- the natural spaces in your area
- your opinion of recycling with reasons
- how you travelled around your town last week
- what you will do to help protect the environment in future.

Write your answer **in Spanish**. You should aim to write between 80 and 90 words. *[18 marks]*

WRITING

Foundation

4 Describe the photo.
Write four short sentences **in Spanish**.

4a .... *[2 marks]*

4b .... *[2 marks]*

4c .... *[2 marks]*

4d .... *[2 marks]*

READING

Higher

5 Read Juan's description of the environmental problems in his town.

> Hay demasiada polución en mi ciudad. Pasearía al lado del río, pero el humo que produce la fábrica cercana me hace sentirme enfermo. Además, ese río está lleno de basura de mi ciudad y los peces no pueden sobrevivir.
>
> Antes paseaba en el bosque, pero ya no puedo. Una compañía lo compró para construir un centro comercial. Ya no es precioso sino una zona de construcción.

Put a cross in each one of the **three** correct boxes.

Juan says that...

	A the factory produces a lot of rubbish.
	B smoke makes him feel ill.
	C the river is at risk of flooding.
	D rubbish is killing animals.
	E a company built a sports centre.
	F the forest used to be beautiful.

[3 marks]

Score:

Equality and Social Issues

READING

Foundation

1a Read Hugo's blog post about social issues.

> *Me pongo enfadado cuando alguien tira comida. Hay gente que no tiene suficiente dinero para comer. En los supermercados la comida cuesta demasiado.*
>
> *Desafortunadamente, también hay gente que tiene frío en sus casas porque la* ***calefacción*** *es demasiado cara. Tienen que llevar chaquetas en casa.*

Complete the sentences below. Put a cross in the correct box for each question.

i) Hugo gets angry when people...

	A buy too much food.
	B can't afford food.
	C throw away food.

[1 mark]

ii) According to the text, supermarkets...

	A are too expensive.
	B waste food.
	C help people.

[1 mark]

1b Which of these is the best translation of the word ***calefacción***?

Put a cross in the correct box.

	A heating
	B furniture
	C fridge

[1 mark]

LISTENING

2 A newsreader is reading the headlines.
What does she mention?
Listen to the recording and put a cross in each one of the **three** correct boxes.

Listening Track 25

	A violence
	B hunger
	C unemployment
	D equal pay
	E crime
	F transport

[3 marks]

SPEAKING

3 Choose **one** of the pictures below to describe.
Make notes on it to use during the test.

Speaking Track 10

Example Answer Video

Your teacher will ask you to describe the picture. You should talk for approximately **one and a half to two minutes**. Your description must cover the **people, location and activity** shown in the picture.

After you have spoken about the content of the picture, your teacher will ask you two questions about your chosen picture. Then, they will ask you some questions related to any of the topics within the theme of **My Neighbourhood**.

Higher

Picture 1

Picture 2

[28 marks]

WRITING

4 Translate the following paragraph **into English**.

Higher

I love our multicultural world, but unfortunately it isn't equal. Equality is a topic that matters to me a lot. A recent article said that most people know a victim of discrimination. For me, it is necessary to teach everyone how to improve society and make it equal. We have more power if we work together.

[10 marks]

Score:

Technology, The Internet and Streaming

SPEAKING

Foundation

1 Nadim has written a social media post about technology. Read out the text below to your teacher.

Speaking Track 11

Example Answer Video

No puedo vivir sin tecnología.

Todas las noches juego con la videoconsola.

En las redes sociales, puedo mandar mensajes.

Hay mucha información útil en Internet.

Intento apagar mi móvil cuando me voy a la cama.

- Once you have read the text, you will then be asked two questions related to what you have read.
- You are expected to say a few words or a short phrase/sentence in response to each question. One-word answers will not be sufficient to gain full marks.

[12 marks]

LISTENING

2 Luisa is talking about how she uses the Internet. What does she say? Listen to the recording and complete the following tables **in English**. You do not need to write in full sentences.

Listening Track 26

Foundation

2a

Internet activity she does in the evening
....

[1 mark]

2b

Something she buys online
....

[1 mark]

2c

Reason she is unhappy
....

[1 mark]

Higher

2d

Way she will protect her information
....

[1 mark]

WRITING

3 Write to your friend about the Internet. You **must** include the following points:

- when you use the Internet
- your opinion of streaming with reasons
- something you used a computer for recently
- what you will do online next week.

Write your answer **in Spanish**. You should aim to write between 80 and 90 words. *[18 marks]*

READING

4 Read Alejandro's article about technology for a Spanish magazine.

Debido a la llegada del Internet, nuestros estilos de vida han cambiado enormemente durante los últimos años. Para alguna gente, ha sido difícil adaptarse a todos los cambios. Por eso, el gobierno español acaba de crear un programa especial para reducir el miedo que ciertas personas tienen de la tecnología. Se ofrecerá a las personas mayores de dieciocho años la oportunidad de asistir a clases en su barrio para aprender sobre el mundo complicado del Internet. Si las clases tienen éxito, se creará un curso específicamente para niños en el futuro.

Los alumnos aprenderán a usar páginas web para hacer búsquedas y encontrar información, hacer las compras en Internet, y enviar y recibir correos electrónicos. Además, habrá tareas para entregar al profesor durante el curso. Cuando haga la última clase del curso, cada alumno recibirá un título virtual para mostrar sus capacidades en el uso de Internet.

Answer the following questions **in English**. You do not need to write in full sentences.

Higher

4a What has happened recently because of the Internet?

.... *[1 mark]*

4b What is the government's objective?

.... *[1 mark]*

4c Who can attend the workshops?

.... *[1 mark]*

4d Name **one** skill the course will help participants develop.

.... *[1 mark]*

4e What will participants be given at the end of the course?

.... *[1 mark]*

Score:

Social Media

WRITING

Foundation

1 Write an article about a social media app you use.
You **must** include the following points:

- a description of what you do on the app
- your opinion of the app
- what you will next use the app for.

Write your answer **in Spanish**. You should aim to write between 40 and 50 words. *[14 marks]*

LISTENING

Foundation

Listening Track 27

2 Monika is asking for details about a new social media app.
What does she find out?
Listen to the recording and complete the following tables **in English**.
You do not need to write in full sentences.

2a

How to contact someone in the app
....

[1 mark]

2b

What you can share with followers
....

[1 mark]

2c

What you can do about comments
....

[1 mark]

READING

3 Read Iván's message about his usage of social media.

Example Answer Video

En el pasado tenía más de diez cuentas en las redes sociales, pero recientemente he cerrado la mayoría. He subido muchas publicaciones en los últimos meses pero he recibido pocos mensajes y ahora estoy aburrido. La verdad es que me gustaría pasar menos tiempo en línea porque es más saludable hacer otras actividades.

Complete the gap in each sentence using a word from the box below.
There are more words than gaps.

accounts	posts	messages	photos
boring	healthy	exciting	

3a Iván has deleted a lot of his .... *[1 mark]*

3b He doesn't have many .... *[1 mark]*

3c Spending more time offline will be .... *[1 mark]*

LISTENING

Higher

4 Javier and Gaby are talking about the advantages and disadvantages of social media. What do they say?

Listening Track 28

Listen to the podcast and complete the following tables **in English**.
You do not need to write in full sentences.

4a Javier

Advantage	....
Disadvantage	....

[1 mark]

[1 mark]

4b Gaby

Advantage	....
Disadvantage	....

[1 mark]

[1 mark]

Score:

Mixed Practice — Foundation

WRITING

Foundation

1 Translate the following five sentences **into Spanish**.

1a I like to use streaming services.

....

.... *[2 marks]*

1b They are useful for downloading music.

....

.... *[2 marks]*

1c I share songs on social networks.

....

.... *[2 marks]*

1d I also make content with my friends online.

....

.... *[2 marks]*

1e Last month we uploaded a funny video.

....

.... *[2 marks]*

WRITING

Foundation

2 Write an article about your local area.
You **must** include the following points:

- description of your local area
- your opinion of the shops there
- what you will do in your neighbourhood next week.

Write your answer **in Spanish**. You should aim to write between 40 and 50 words. *[14 marks]*

READING

Foundation

3 Read Jalil's email.

> *Uso mucho Internet. Me gusta leer blogs de viajes y ver vídeos de naturaleza. Recibo correos electrónicos de mi amigo mexicano y él me manda fotos de su pueblo. Las bajo en mi móvil. Nunca compro regalos en línea porque prefiero ir a las tiendas.*

Put a cross in each one of the **three** correct boxes.

Jalil...

	A writes travel blogs.
	B watches nature videos.
	C receives emails from his friend.
	D downloads photos on his tablet.
	E prefers to shop online.
	F likes going to shops.

[3 marks]

LISTENING

Foundation

4 Carmen is talking about caring for the environment at home. What does she say? Listen to the recording and complete the sentences by putting a cross in the correct box for each question.

Listening Track 29

4a Carmen thinks that recycling is...

	A difficult.
	B essential.
	C expensive.

[1 mark]

4b She always recycles her...

	A clothes.
	B paper.
	C plastic.

[1 mark]

4c Her family prepares meals with...

	A home-grown vegetables.
	B only vegan food.
	C local seafood.

[1 mark]

4d They grow flowers in their garden for...

	A their neighbours.
	B town markets.
	C local wildlife.

[1 mark]

SPEAKING

5 Choose **one** of the pictures below to describe.
Make notes on it to use during the test.

Speaking Track 12

Your teacher will ask you to describe the picture. You should talk for approximately **one and a half to two minutes**. Your description must cover the **people, location and activity** shown in the picture.

After you have spoken about the content of the picture, your teacher will ask you two questions about your chosen picture. Then, they will ask you some questions related to any of the topics within the theme of **Media and technology.**

Foundation

Picture 1

Picture 2

[28 marks]

WRITING

6 Translate the following five sentences **into Spanish**.

Foundation

6a I want to make a difference in the world.

....

.... *[2 marks]*

6b Hunger is a problem in my neighbourhood.

....

.... *[2 marks]*

6c I go to a young person's club in order to help others.

....

.... *[2 marks]*

6d Yesterday we cooked meals for our community.

....

.... *[2 marks]*

READING

Foundation

7 Read these forum posts from young people about changes to where they live.

Sasha : *Han puesto bancos y equipo deportivo en los parques de mi pueblo. Ahora hay más que hacer cuando hace buen tiempo. Así también la gente disfrutará más de estar al aire libre.*

Mario : *Mi pueblo ha mejorado las calles del centro para hacerlo una zona más segura. También ha limpiado la plaza mayor para hacerla un sitio más bonito.*

Nadia : *En mi barrio abrimos un jardín público para tener un nuevo espacio para eventos en la comunidad. También pusimos flores fuera de edificios y esto ha hecho el pueblo más verde.*

Complete the following tables **in English**.

You do not need to write in full sentences.

7a Sasha

One improvement in her town	....
One reason	....

[1 mark]

[1 mark]

7b Mario

One improvement in his town	....
One reason	....

[1 mark]

[1 mark]

7c Nadia

One improvement in her town	....
One reason	....

[1 mark]

[1 mark]

Score:

Mixed Practice — Both Tiers

1 David is talking about technology in a podcast. What does he say?
Complete the gap in each sentence using a word or phrase from the box below.
There are more words/phrases than gaps.

Listening Track 30

fast	old	expensive	broken
laptop	tablet	mobile phone	
film	series	match	video

1a David's laptop is .... *[1 mark]*

1b The radio is .... *[1 mark]*

1c He listens to songs on his .... *[1 mark]*

1d This weekend he and his friend will watch a .... *[1 mark]*

1e He's going to sit through a .... alone. *[1 mark]*

2 You are in a shopping centre in Spain and stop at the information desk.
Listen to the recording to hear the part of the teacher. They will speak first.

Speaking Track 13

- Your teacher will ask questions **in Spanish** and you must answer **in Spanish**.
- You are expected to say a few words or a short phrase / sentence in response to each prompt. One-word answers will not be sufficient to gain full marks.

Task:

1. Say what kind of shop you are looking for.
2. Say what you would like to buy.
3. Say why you are visiting the region.
4. Give your opinion of the local area.
5. Ask a question about the town centre.

[10 marks]

READING

3a Read Karima's article on what her school is doing to help the environment.

> Mi colegio ha hecho mucho para ser más responsable con el medio ambiente en los últimos cuatro meses. Comenzó con grupos de alumnos y profesores trabajando juntos para proteger la naturaleza en nuestro patio y campo.
>
> Ahora estamos intentando reciclar papel y apagar los ordenadores al final del día. La directora recomienda caminar al colegio y pronto hará una presentación sobre cambios de estilo de vida **sostenibles***. El colegio dejará de usar cosas peligrosas para el planeta. Por ejemplo, las botellas de plástico que pueden ser ***nocivas*** para los animales cuando la gente las tira sin reciclarlas.
>
> **sostenibles* = sustainable

Complete the sentences below. Put a cross in the correct box for each question.

i) Her school started making changes...

	A four weeks ago.
	B several months ago.
	C last year.

[1 mark]

ii) Her school has been helping nature in...

	A their outdoor spaces.
	B public places nearby.
	C the countryside.

[1 mark]

iii) Students are making an effort to...

	A recycle plastics in class.
	B switch off computers.
	C not use as much paper.

[1 mark]

iv) The head teacher will...

	A walk to school.
	B make new sustainability rules.
	C talk to students about lifestyle choices.

[1 mark]

3b Which of these is the best translation of the word ***nocivas***?
Put a cross in the correct box.

	A harmful
	B flimsy
	C overpriced

[1 mark]

Score:

Mixed Practice — Higher

LISTENING

Higher

1 Amira, Jorge and Sebastian are talking about the advantages and disadvantages of living with other people. What do they say?

Listening Track 31

Listen to the recording and complete the following tables **in English**. You do not need to write in full sentences.

1a Amira

Advantage	....
Disadvantage	....

[1 mark]

[1 mark]

1b Jorge

Advantage	....
Disadvantage	....

[1 mark]

[1 mark]

1c Sebastian

Advantage	....
Disadvantage	....

[1 mark]

[1 mark]

WRITING

Higher

2 Translate the following paragraph **into Spanish**.

Example Answer Video

I posted a new video on the Internet last week. It was about security on social networks. For me, these networks are convenient for communicating with my friends. However, there are dangers and it's important to teach people how to avoid them. The video created an interesting discussion among my followers.

....

....

....

....

.... *[10 marks]*

SPEAKING

Speaking Track 14

3 You are at an electronics shop in Spain and you are talking to an employee. Listen to the recording to hear the part of the teacher. They will speak first.

- Your teacher will ask questions **in Spanish** and you must answer **in Spanish**.
- You are expected to say a few words or a short phrase / sentence in response to each prompt. One-word answers will not be sufficient to gain full marks.

Higher

Task:

1. Say what kind of device you want to buy.
2. Say what features you would like it to have.
3. Say what you will use the device for.
4. Ask a question about the cost.
5. Ask a question about something else you want to buy.

[10 marks]

READING

4a Read Cris's blog post.

Mi novia y yo vivíamos en la misma ciudad, pero me mudé de la región por mi trabajo y ahora alquilo un piso en el norte del país. Ella se quedó en el sur y la visito a menudo.*

Un día, nos gustaría tener nuestra propia casa. Queremos que tenga una cocina enorme y una biblioteca llena de libros antiguos. Además, mi novia es artista y trabaja con el vidrio, entonces querrá un ***taller*** *en el jardín. Será un sitio perfecto para sus proyectos.*

**me mudé = I moved (out)*

Answer the following questions **in English**.
You do not need to write in full sentences.

Higher

i) Where does Cris's girlfriend live? (1 detail)

.... *[1 mark]*

ii) What do the couple want inside their ideal house? (1 detail)

.... *[1 mark]*

4b Which of these is the best translation of the word ***taller***?

Put a cross in the correct box.

	A nursery
	B greenhouse
	C workshop

[1 mark]

LISTENING

5a Listen to Andrea's podcast about social problems. What does she say?
Listen to the recording and put a cross in each one of the **three** correct boxes.

Listening Track 32

	A Rich people can also have financial worries.
	B There is a huge gap between rich and poorer people.
	C We should make basic necessities more affordable.
	D We should all donate more food and clothing.
	E People often waste money on things they don't need.
	F People could support their lives better with more money.

[3 marks]

Higher

5b Andrea now shares some information about local crime.
Listen to the recording, then answer the questions **in English**.
You do not need to write in full sentences.

i) What has happened to crime in Andrea's area?

.... *[1 mark]*

ii) Which group of people have the criminals angered?

.... *[1 mark]*

iii) According to Andrea, what is the community doing to combat the problem?

....

.... *[1 mark]*

SPEAKING

6 Fátima has contributed to a blog about charity work.
Read out the text below to your teacher.

Speaking Track 15

Higher

> Ayudo a una organización local que organiza campañas sociales.
>
> Informamos a los ciudadanos sobre los problemas que están afectando a las personas sin hogar.
>
> Además, se empieza a recoger ropa y comida para esa gente.
>
> También doy dinero a otras dos asociaciones que luchan por la igualdad de género.

- Once you have read the text, you will then be asked two questions related to what you have read.
- You are expected to say a few words or a short phrase/sentence in response to each question. One-word answers will not be sufficient to gain full marks.

[12 marks]

READING

7 Read this post about the local environment from a Spanish town council's website.

> *El peor problema en nuestro pueblo es la basura en las playas. Ha causado un daño grave a las especies de animales en esas zonas. Vamos a publicar un panfleto* virtual para informar a los habitantes. Esto debería animarles a mantener limpios los espacios naturales.*
>
> *Además, queremos reducir la polución del aire. Entonces, gastaremos más dinero en transporte público para proporcionar una alternativa al coche.*
>
> **panfleto = leaflet*

What does the post tell us?
Complete the tables **in English**. You do not need to write in full sentences.

Higher

7a

The town's worst problem
....

[1 mark]

7b

The impact on local wildlife
....

[1 mark]

7c

What the leaflet will encourage locals to do
....

[1 mark]

7d

The council's plan to tackle air pollution
....

[1 mark]

WRITING

8 Write a blog about social media.
You **must** include the following points:

Higher

- how you normally use social media
- the pros and cons of online communication
- a recent interaction you had online
- how you think social media will change in the future.

Write your answer **in Spanish**.
You should aim to write between 130 and 150 words. *[22 marks]*

Score:

School Subjects and School Life

LISTENING

1 Monika is talking about her life at school. What does she say?
Listen to the recording, then answer the questions **in English**.
You do not need to write in full sentences.

Listening Track 33

Foundation

i) Which subject does Monika enjoy the most?

.... *[1 mark]*

ii) What does Monika say about her school's facilities? Give one detail.

.... *[1 mark]*

WRITING

2 Write an email to your Cuban friend about your school.
You **must** include the following points:

- what your teachers are like
- your opinion of a school subject with reasons
- what you studied at school last week
- which club(s) you would like to become a member of in the future.

Write your answer **in Spanish**. You should aim to write between 80 and 90 words. *[18 marks]*

READING

Higher

3 Translate the following paragraph **into English**.

> Asisto a mi instituto actual desde hace dos años. Mi último era maravilloso y me encantó estudiar allí. Por lo tanto, fue duro cambiar de escuelas y venir aquí. Ahora disfruto de mis clases y sigo haciendo amistades con mis compañeros. Además, estudiamos varios idiomas, lo que me interesa muchísimo.

....

....

....

....

....

.... *[10 marks]*

SPEAKING

4 Jorge, your Chilean friend, has written to you about their life at school. Read out the text below to your teacher.

Scan the QR code to hear the teacher part of the question, or you can find the transcript in the back of the book.

Speaking Track 16

Foundation

Llego al instituto a las ocho y diez.
La primera clase del día es la religión.
Es una de mis asignaturas favoritas.
También me encanta la educación física porque soy activo.
Nuestro instituto tiene un patio muy grande para practicar deportes.

- Once you have read the text, you will then be asked two questions related to what you have read.
- You are expected to say a few words or a short phrase/sentence in response to each question. One-word answers will not be sufficient to gain full marks.

[12 marks]

LISTENING

5 You are going to hear someone talking about their school.

Listening Track 34

Sentences 1 and 3: Write down the missing words in the gaps provided. In each gap, you will write one word **in Spanish**.

Sentences 2 and 4: Write down the full sentences that you hear in the spaces provided, **in Spanish**.

Higher

5a **Sentence 1**

El .... en mi .... es .... *[2 marks]*

5b **Sentence 2**

....

.... *[2 marks]*

5c **Sentence 3**

El .... para .... el .... es estricto. *[2 marks]*

5d **Sentence 4**

....

.... *[2 marks]*

Score:

School Pressures and Difficulties

READING

Foundation

1a Read Marta's blog post about some difficulties at school.

> *Me preparo mucho para los exámenes porque quiero sacar buenas notas. No me gusta la historia porque encuentro las clases aburridas, pero me encantan las de las ciencias. Entonces, las estudio hasta tarde en casa y no me duermo fácilmente. Necesito más descanso porque tener poco sueño me deja **agotada**.*

Complete the sentences below. Put a cross in the correct box for each question.

i) Marta wants to...

	A take exams early.
	B have fewer classes.
	C get good grades.

[1 mark]

ii) She also says she...

	A stays at school after her lessons.
	B enjoys her science classes.
	C wants to study history more.

[1 mark]

1b Which of these is the best translation of the word ***agotada***?

Put a cross in the correct box.

	A bored
	B excited
	C exhausted

[1 mark]

LISTENING

2 Alba is talking about different issues at school.
What does she mention?
Listen to the recording and put a cross in each one of the **three** correct boxes.

Listening Track 35

	A Class presentations
	B School rules
	C Uniform
	D Exams
	E Teachers
	F Homework

[3 marks]

WRITING

Higher

3 Write about school pressures for an online magazine.
You **must** include the following points:

- the behaviour in your school
- the pros and cons of class discussions
- a deadline you had recently
- how you will prepare for future exams.

Write your answer **in Spanish**.
You should aim to write between 130 and 150 words. *[22 marks]*

READING

4 Read this blog post on a school's website.
Some teachers are giving their students study advice.

Example Answer Video

> *Si te preocupas por los exámenes, primero deberías hablar con alguien sobre tus sentimientos. No tienes que sufrir en silencio porque los profesores te podrán ayudar.*
>
> *"Mientras te preparas para los exámenes, estudiar con tus amigos será muy útil porque así podréis compartir ideas," recomendó una profesora.*
>
> *Otro explicó la importancia de* ***ordenar*** *bien tu espacio. "Mantenerlo limpio es importante porque no se puede estudiar cuando hay papeles por todas partes," dijo él.*

Higher

4a Answer the following questions **in English**. You do not need to write in full sentences.

i) According to the post, what is the best thing you can do if you're struggling?

.... *[1 mark]*

ii) According to one of the teachers, why is group work useful?

.... *[1 mark]*

4b Which of these is the best translation of the word ***ordenar***?

Put a cross in the correct box.

	A to select
	B to tidy
	C to decorate

[1 mark]

Score:

Education Post-16 and Career Choices & Ambitions

SPEAKING

Foundation

1 Choose **one** of the pictures below to describe.
Make notes on it to use during the test.

Speaking Track 17

Your teacher will ask you to describe the picture. You should talk for approximately **one and a half to two minutes**. Your description must cover the **people, location and activity** shown in the picture.

After you have spoken about the content of the picture, your teacher will ask you two questions about your chosen picture. Then, they will ask you some questions related to any of the topics within the theme of **Studying and My Future**.

Picture 1

Picture 2

[28 marks]

LISTENING

2 Ana wants to apply to be a police officer.
What does she find out?
Listen to the recording and complete the following tables **in English**.
You do not need to write in full sentences.

Listening Track 36

2a

Qualifications
....

[1 mark]

2b

Working hours
....

[1 mark]

2c

Positive impact of the job
....

[1 mark]

WRITING

Foundation

3 Write an article about a job you know of. You **must** include the following points:

- a description of the job
- your opinion of this job
- what you will do after leaving school.

Write your answer **in Spanish**. You should aim to write between 40 and 50 words. *[14 marks]*

READING

Higher

4 Read Jorge and Andrea's forum posts about their future plans.

4a

Jorge: No sé si quiero ir a la universidad después de terminar el colegio, pero estoy pensando en viajar durante un año. Me gustaría recorrer el mundo y conocer la vida en otros países. Además, ya que todavía me falta elegir una carrera, creo que podría usar ese año para buscar experiencia laboral. Eso me ayudaría a decidir lo que quiero hacer en el futuro.

Put a cross next to each one of the **two** correct statements.

Jorge says that...

	A he will go to university.
	B he wants to experience other cultures.
	C he's thinking of doing work experience.
	D he's decided the career he wants to do.

[2 marks]

4b

Andrea: Cuando era pequeña quería ser cantante, pero cambié mis planes porque me sentía muy nerviosa cuando cantaba en público. Ahora me interesa ser artista profesional. Por lo tanto, voy a cambiar de colegio el año que viene. Iré a una escuela especial para conseguir una formación en arte. Tendré que crear mi propia exposición que será juzgada por expertos.

What does Andrea tell us?

Complete the tables **in English**. You do not need to write in full sentences.

i)

Why she changed her career path
....

[1 mark]

ii)

What she will do next year (1 detail)
....

[1 mark]

iii)

Her exhibition
....

[1 mark]

Score:

Where to Go and Accommodation & Travel

WRITING

Foundation

1 Translate the following five sentences **into Spanish**.

1a I go to Spain every summer.

....

.... *[2 marks]*

1b My family catches the plane.

....

.... *[2 marks]*

1c We visit tranquil villages near to the coast.

....

.... *[2 marks]*

1d I love spending time outdoors.

....

.... *[2 marks]*

1e On our last trip my aunt rented a car.

....

.... *[2 marks]*

WRITING

2 Write an email to your friend about your holiday activities.
You **must** include the following points:

- what you like to do on holiday
- your opinion of camping with reasons
- where you spent your last holiday
- what you will do on holiday next year.

Write your answer **in Spanish**. You should aim to write between 80 and 90 words. *[18 marks]*

LISTENING

Listening Track 37

Foundation

3 Dolores is talking about her current holiday. What does she say? Listen to the recording and complete the sentences by putting a cross in the correct box for each question.

3a The hotel is...

	A old.
	B cheap.
	C modern.

[1 mark]

3b The room has a view of...

	A the park.
	B the sea.
	C the beach.

[1 mark]

3c She wants to...

	A go shopping.
	B take pictures.
	C visit a museum.

[1 mark]

SPEAKING

Speaking Track 18

Example Answer Video

Higher

4 You are in a hotel and want to ask about getting around the area. Listen to the recording to hear the part of the receptionist. They will speak first.

- Your teacher will ask questions **in Spanish** and you must answer **in Spanish**.
- You are expected to say a few words or a short phrase / sentence in response to each prompt. One-word answers will not be sufficient to gain full marks.

Task:

1. Say where you want to go today.
2. Say what type of transport you will take.
3. Ask a question about transport tickets.
4. Say what you think about the hotel.
5. Ask a question about meals in the hotel.

[10 marks]

Score:

Tourist Attractions

READING

Foundation

1 Read these comments from Alba and Juan. Complete the following tables **in English**. You do not need to write in full sentences.

Alba: Cada año en mi pueblo tenemos siete ferias y celebramos muchas tradiciones. Creo que son importantes. Es emocionante preparar comida y siempre tengo ganas de participar en bailes.

1a

One detail about where she lives	....
One activity she likes	....

[1 mark]

[1 mark]

Juan: Mi familia pasa la mayoría de los días de fiesta en casa. Yo prefiero celebrarlos con mis amigos en la plaza o en la playa. Esta primavera pasaré el festival de Carnaval en otra ciudad.

1b

One place he likes to be on festival days	....
What he will celebrate elsewhere	....

[1 mark]

[1 mark]

LISTENING

2 Pilar is talking about what tourists should see in her city. What does she say? Complete the gap in each sentence using a word or phrase from the box below. There are more words/phrases than gaps.

Listening Track 38

museum	palace	castle	monument
boat ride	famous café	city bus tour	
food	souvenirs	maps	tickets

2a The first thing you should see is the .... *[1 mark]*

2b The .... will close soon. *[1 mark]*

2c Pilar recommends a .... *[1 mark]*

2d The market is famous for its .... *[1 mark]*

2e Near the square you can get .... *[1 mark]*

WRITING

Higher

3 Write a blog about tourism.
You **must** include the following points:

- what you enjoy doing on holiday
- the pros and cons of being a tourist
- a tourist attraction you visited in the past
- a cultural activity you will try on your next holiday.

Write your answer **in Spanish**.
You should aim to write between 130 and 150 words. *[22 marks]*

LISTENING

Higher

4 A museum guide is talking about the Day of the Dead. What does he say?
Listen to the recording and complete the sentences by putting a cross in the correct box for each question.

Listening Track 39

4a This tradition is celebrated...

	A in the middle of November.
	B at the beginning of November.
	C at the end of November.

[1 mark]

4b The photos show people...

	A dressing up.
	B cooking special foods.
	C selling gifts.

[1 mark]

4c According to the guide, the customs are...

	A practised in many countries.
	B still practised now.
	C practised all year round.

[1 mark]

4d The guide says you will also see people...

	A buying traditional food.
	B tidying up their shops.
	C making offerings.

[1 mark]

Score:

Mixed Practice — Foundation

READING

Foundation

1 Read these comments from an online article.

Raúl: Quiero ser profesor en el futuro. Este verano busco experiencia trabajando con niños.

Lola: Me encanta el ciclismo y tengo planes para abrir una tienda de bicicletas. Quisiera tener mi propia empresa.

Iván: Trabajar en el turismo es mi sueño. Entonces, me gustaría ir a la universidad para estudiar lenguas.

Who says what? Choose the correct answers.
Put a cross in the correct column for each question.

	Who...	**Raúl**	**Lola**	**Iván**
a)	...loves cycling?			
b)	...is looking for work experience?			
c)	...would like to have their own business?			
d)	...dreams of working in tourism?			
e)	...wants to be a teacher?			
f)	...wants to go to university?			

[1 mark]
[1 mark]
[1 mark]
[1 mark]
[1 mark]
[1 mark]

SPEAKING

Foundation

2 Choose **one** of the pictures below to describe.
Make notes on it to use during the test.

Speaking Track 19

Example Answer Video

Your teacher will ask you to describe the picture. You should talk for approximately **one and a half to two minutes**. Your description must cover the **people, location and activity** shown in the picture.

After you have spoken about the content of the picture, your teacher will ask you two questions about your chosen picture. Then, they will ask you some questions related to any of the topics within the theme of **Travel and Tourism**.

Picture 1

Picture 2

[28 marks]

LISTENING

Foundation

3 Listen to this advert promoting Cádiz. What is mentioned?
Listen to the recording and put a cross in each one of the **three** correct boxes.

Listening Track 40

	A museums
	B the weather
	C local traditions
	D places to stay
	E food and drink
	F transport

[3 marks]

WRITING

Foundation

4 Translate the following five sentences **into Spanish**.

4a I go to an international school.

....

.... *[2 marks]*

4b There are only three hundred pupils.

....

.... *[2 marks]*

4c I enjoy my classes because they are small.

....

.... *[2 marks]*

4d Last week I had a lot of science homework.

....

.... *[2 marks]*

4e If I get good grades, I can go to university.

....

.... *[2 marks]*

LISTENING

5 Emilio is talking about his career plans. What does he say? Listen to the recording and complete the sentences by putting a cross in the correct box for each question.

Listening Track 41

5a Emilio wants to work as a...

	A police officer.
	B doctor.
	C professor.

[1 mark]

5b A positive aspect of the job is the...

	A holidays.
	B hours.
	C salary.

[1 mark]

Foundation

5c To get the job, Emilio has to...

	A complete a project.
	B go to university.
	C study abroad.

[1 mark]

5d He is currently looking for...

	A work experience.
	B a summer job.
	C the best course.

[1 mark]

WRITING

6 Write an article about your school.
You **must** include the following points:

Foundation

- a description of your school uniform
- your opinion of your school
- what you will study next week.

Write your answer **in Spanish**. You should aim to write between 40 and 50 words. *[14 marks]*

Score:

Mixed Practice — Both Tiers

SPEAKING

1 You are at a tourist office in Spain, and you are talking to an employee. Listen to the recording to hear the part of the teacher. They will speak first.

Speaking Track 20

- Your teacher will ask questions **in Spanish** and you must answer **in Spanish**.
- You are expected to say a few words or a short phrase / sentence in response to each prompt. One-word answers will not be sufficient to gain full marks.

Task:

1. Give a tourist attraction you would like to visit.
2. Say when you want to go.
3. Say where your hotel is.
4. Say what type of transport you prefer.
5. Ask a question about buying tickets.

[10 marks]

READING

2 Read Leya's email to a pen pal about her school.

Las clases comienzan a las nueve menos diez. Tenemos seis clases cada día y tenemos una hora para comer. A menudo tenemos una asignatura dura por la tarde, como matemáticas o ciencias. Creo que sería mejor tener menos tiempo para comer y volver a casa más temprano.

Complete the sentences below. Put a cross in the correct box for each question.

2a Classes start at...

	A ten to nine.
	B nine o'clock.
	C ten past nine.

[1 mark]

2b Leya thinks that maths is...

	A more useful than science.
	B better in the afternoon.
	C a difficult subject.

[1 mark]

2c Leya wishes that she could...

	A have shorter lunch breaks.
	B start school earlier.
	C go home for lunch.

[1 mark]

LISTENING

3 An office manager is giving information to a new team of employees. What does she mention? Listen to the recording and put a cross in each one of the **three** correct boxes.

Listening Track 42

	A uniform
	B holidays
	C working hours
	D salary
	E travel discounts
	F free food

[3 marks]

READING

4 Read this article about a Spanish sports event.

A finales de abril se celebra el Maratón de Madrid. Este año, miles de personas participaron y viajaron desde países de todo el mundo. El evento siempre comienza en el centro y pasa por varios sitios históricos. Si visitas Madrid durante el maratón, escucharás música en las calles porque grupos musicales organizan conciertos para los turistas.

4a Complete the sentences below. Put a cross in the correct box for each question.

i) The race takes place...

	A throughout April.
	B at the start of April.
	C at the end of April.

[1 mark]

ii) This year, race participants came from...

	A the capital city.
	B all over the world.
	C thousands of organisations.

[1 mark]

4b Answer the following questions **in English**.
You do not need to write in full sentences.

i) What does the marathon take runners past?

.... *[1 mark]*

ii) During the event, who do bands play for?

.... *[1 mark]*

LISTENING

5 Gaby is talking about loneliness at school. What does she say? Listen to the recording and complete the sentences by putting a cross in the correct box for each question.

Listening Track 43

5a Gaby's classmate...

	A wants to help others.
	B is nervous to talk to others.
	C has been a victim of bullying.

[1 mark]

5b Gaby decided to...

	A talk with her teacher.
	B befriend the classmate.
	C create a lunchtime club.

[1 mark]

5c Now, students can...

	A leave school at lunch.
	B eat in a quieter area.
	C talk to teachers during lunch.

[1 mark]

LISTENING

6 Hugo and Luis are talking about the hotels they are staying in on holiday. What do they like and dislike? Complete the following tables **in English**. You do not need to write in full sentences.

Listening Track 44

6a Hugo...

likes...	....
dislikes...	....

[1 mark]

[1 mark]

6b Luis...

likes...	....
dislikes...	....

[1 mark]

[1 mark]

READING

7a Read Nadim's school report about his work experience.

> *El año pasado hice experiencia de trabajo. Escogí un centro deportivo porque no quería trabajar en una oficina. Disfrutaba ayudando en clases de deporte. Pero estaba cansado porque estuve de pie todo el tiempo .*
>
> *Ahora estoy pensando en mi futuro. Todavía no sé exactamente qué quiero hacer pero ir a la universidad me interesa. Quisiera un buen salario, pero ser feliz me importa igualmente.*
>
> *Me encanta escribir y sería guay hacerlo en el trabajo. También encuentro emocionante conocer las noticias del mundo, entonces creo que me gustaría ser* ***periodista****.*

Complete the sentences below. Put a cross in the correct box for each question.

i) Nadim did work experience in...

	A an office.
	B a primary school.
	C a sports centre.

[1 mark]

ii) He was...

	A helping out at reception.
	B always on his feet.
	C leading classes.

[1 mark]

iii) Nadim...

	A wants more work experience.
	B knows what career he wants.
	C is interested in university.

[1 mark]

iv) For him...

	A a good salary is important.
	B travelling for work is ideal.
	C happiness is what matters most.

[1 mark]

7b Which of these is the best translation of the word ***periodista***?
Put a cross in the correct box.

	A journalist
	B travel agent
	C politician

[1 mark]

Score:

Mixed Practice — Higher

READING

Higher

1 Translate the following paragraph **into English**.

> Después de mis exámenes, quisiera conseguir experiencia laboral. Ya he solicitado puestos en tres empresas en mi región. Ayer tuve una entrevista por teléfono con la directora de una de estas compañías. Pienso que respondí bien a sus preguntas y me siento muy optimista de recibir una oferta. Trabajar allí sería una oportunidad excelente.

....

....

....

....

....

....

.... *[10 marks]*

SPEAKING

Higher

2 Choose **one** of the pictures below to describe.
Make notes on it to use during the test.

Speaking Track 21

Your teacher will ask you to describe the picture. You should talk for approximately **one and a half to two minutes**. Your description must cover the **people, location and activity** shown in the picture.

After you have spoken about the content of the picture, your teacher will ask you two questions about your chosen picture. Then, they will ask you some questions related to any of the topics within the theme of **Studying and my future**.

Picture 1

Picture 2

[28 marks]

WRITING

Higher

3 Write a blog about the world of work. You **must** include the following points:

Example Answer Video

- a job that one of your friends has
- the pros and cons of working in an office
- what work experience you have done in the past
- what work experience you would like to do in the future.

Write your answer **in Spanish**.
You should aim to write between 130 and 150 words. *[22 marks]*

LISTENING

Higher

4 Lin is discussing his future. What does he say? Complete the gap in each sentence using a word or phrase from the box below. There are more words/phrases than gaps.

Listening Track 45

travel	go to university	do something practical	leave home
mechanic	police officer	scientist	
happiness	future career	degree	salary

4a In the future, Lin would like to .... *[1 mark]*

4b His mother says he should .... *[1 mark]*

4c His mother wanted to become a .... *[1 mark]*

4d Lin thinks that his .... is less important than his .... *[2 marks]*

WRITING

Higher

5 Translate the following paragraph **into Spanish**.

When I go abroad, I love flying. Planes are the fastest way to travel and the views are incredible. I enjoy all types of transport, except for boats. They usually make me feel sick and I hate the smell of salt. It's worth it to try different travel experiences because they are all unique.

....

....

....

....

.... *[10 marks]*

READING

6 Read Lola's blog post about her recent holiday.

Acabo de volver del campo con mis amigos. Hicimos muchas actividades que no es posible hacer en la ciudad, como montar en bicicleta por las montañas y caminar por los bosques. En la ciudad, lo más que puedo hacer es ir al parque.

Lo que más me encanta de este tipo de vacaciones son las opciones para alojamiento. Durante nuestras vacaciones mis amigos y yo nos quedamos en un camping. Había un gran lago cerca y todas las noches cenamos pescado con arroz. Estaba muy rico.

En el campo siempre disfruto de la naturaleza. Durante nuestro viaje vimos varios paisajes preciosos desde la montaña más cercana. Sin embargo, no subimos toda la montaña. Aunque llevamos suficiente agua, estábamos demasiado cansados para continuar.

Quiero intentar subirla otra vez y por lo tanto he reservado mi próximo viaje allí para diciembre. Voy en tren, pero mi llegada dependerá del tiempo en aquel momento.

Answer the following questions **in English**.

You do not need to write in full sentences.

Higher

6a Where did Lola go on holiday?

.... *[1 mark]*

6b What was she able to do that she usually can't? (1 detail)

.... *[1 mark]*

6c What did she eat a lot of?

.... *[1 mark]*

6d What stopped her group from climbing to the top of the mountain?

.... *[1 mark]*

6e Why might she not be able to go on her future trip?

.... *[1 mark]*

Score:

Nouns and Articles

1 Underline all the nouns in the sentences below.

a Odio la historia y el inglés.

b Mi hermano compró unos zapatos nuevos.

c Los deberes son siempre difíciles.

d Tuviste tres bolígrafos rojos.

e Voy a visitar a mi abuelo.

f Me dio un regalo grande.

g Me gustan los gatos y los perros.

h Cada viernes sólo como bocadillos.

i Preferiría ir a la costa que ir al campo.

j Mis padres conocen a mis amigos.

2 Write either **m** or **f** after each noun to show whether it is masculine or feminine.

a sol ....

b playa ....

c teatro ....

d aire ....

e azúcar ....

f actitud ....

g canción ....

h autobús ....

i ciclismo ....

j desayuno ....

k opinión ....

l ciudad ....

m mesa ....

n papel ....

o falda ....

p clase ....

3 Make each of these nouns plural — don't forget to include **los** or **las**.

a verdura ....

b sábado ....

c vez ....

d mes ....

e estadio ....

f jardín ....

g edad ....

h mujer ....

i terror ....

j actriz ....

k voz ....

l jueves ....

m examen ....

n camisa ....

o avión ....

4 Fill in the gaps in these sentences with the plural form of a word from the box. Only use each word **once**.

a Me levanto a las ocho de la mañana todos los ....

b Fui al zoo y vi muchos ....

c Las .... en mi casa son amarillas.

d Tengo un jardín grande con muchas ....

e Mis .... me dan muchos deberes.

profesor
puerta
flor
día
animal

5 Circle the correct definite articles to complete the sentences below.

a **Los** / **Las** chicas juegan al fútbol en el parque.

b **El** / **La** agua está muy limpia.

c Me gustan **la** / **las** noticias.

d **El** / **Los** lunes siempre voy al cine.

e Están en **el** / **la** mismo sitio.

6 Translate these sentences into **Spanish**.

a I hate running because it's hard. ....

b We are learning maths. ....

c The Mexicans prepare wonderful food. ....

d Positivity is important. ....

7 Fill in the gaps in these sentences using the correct indefinite article (**un**, **una**, **unos** or **unas**).

a He comprado .... vestidos, ... camiseta y .... sombrero.

b Tengo .... hermano y .... hermana.

c En mi ciudad, hay .... castillo antiguo y .... plazas grandes.

8 Translate these sentences into **Spanish**.

a He likes eggs and chips.

....

b In the future, she wants to be an artist.

....

c Mrs García is my teacher.

....

d I don't have a computer.

....

Higher

e The best thing is that they are friends.

....

Pronouns

1 Translate these sentences into **Spanish** using the correct subject pronouns.

a I have a dog and you (inf., sing.) have a cat. ....

b You (inf., pl.) can go to the concert. ....

c She is a teacher and he is a singer. ....

d We are here, but they are over there. ....

e You (form., pl.) can leave now. ....

f You (form., sing.) invited Lin to the party. ....

2 Fill in the gaps in these sentences using the correct object pronoun from the box.

a Kazim lava el coche. Kazim .... lava.

b Samira compró una tableta. Samira .... compró.

c Mi primo encontró sus gafas. Mi primo .... encontró.

d La artista pinta estos cuadros. La artista .... pinta.

las
lo
la
los

3 Translate these sentences into **Spanish** using the correct indirect object pronouns.

a He gave me the book. ....

b I sent her a letter. ....

c I called you (inf., sing.) yesterday. ....

d We told them the truth. ....

Higher

4 Circle the correct pronoun in **bold** to complete the sentences below.

a ¿Estas cajas son para **me** / **mí**?

b ¿Ellas irán al evento **con ti** / **contigo**?

c Estábamos hablando de **ti** / **tú** y de **lo** / **él**.

5 Translate these indefinite pronouns into **Spanish**.

a something ....

b everything ....

c someone ....

d some (of them) ....

e none ....

f everyone ....

6 Translate these sentences into **Spanish** using the correct interrogative pronouns.

a Who called you (inf., sing.)? ....

b What are we going to do? ....

c Which one do you (inf., pl.) prefer? ....

d How much does this cost? ....

H **e** Where did they come from? ....

Higher

7 Fill in the gaps in these sentences using the correct relative pronoun from the box.

a De toda mi familia, mi hermano mayor es .... me entiende mejor.

b Mi amigo no dijo nada cuando lo vi, ... me pareció raro.

c El perro .... vimos en el jardín no es el mío.

d Mis padres van a visitar el museo .... he hablado mucho.

e Ayudar a la gente es la razón por .... me gusta ser médico.

que
el que
la cual
lo que
del cual

8 Translate each of these sentences into **English**.

a Esto no me interesa mucho.

....

b ¿Por qué dijiste eso a tu prima?

....

Higher **c** No sabemos qué hacer con aquello.

....

Higher

9 Translate these sentences into **Spanish**. The English nouns in brackets tell you what the possessive pronoun in each sentence is referring to.

Example: Hers is green. (*her house*) *La suya es verde.*

a Mine is blue. (*my T-shirt*) ....

b Yours (inf., sing.) are amusing. (*your games*) ....

c Theirs is quite small. (*their castle*) ....

d Ours are enormous. (*our flowers*) ....

Prepositions and Conjunctions

1 Circle the correct preposition to complete the sentences below.

a Mi colegio está **en** / **desde** Brighton.

b Busco un libro **a** / **sobre** la historia cubana.

c Sus botellas no son **de** / **por** plástico.

d El sábado, queremos ir **a** / **con** la plaza.

e Este autobús va **contra** / **hasta** Wigan.

2 Match each of the following Spanish sentences with its English translation.

a	El gato está al lado de la mesa.	**i**	*The cat is in front of the table.*
b	El gato está delante de la mesa.	**ii**	*The cat is underneath the table.*
c	El gato está debajo de la mesa.	**iii**	*The cat is next to the table.*
d	El gato está detrás de la mesa.	**iv**	*The cat is behind the table.*

3 Translate the prepositions below into **Spanish**.

a	between	....	**d**	except for	....
b	since	....	**e**	towards	....
c	during	....	**f**	inside of	....

Higher (d–f)

4 Translate these sentences into **English**.

a Me gusta correr para estar en forma. ....

b Salen sin coger sus móviles. ....

H c Voy al concierto después de cenar. ....

5 Some of these sentences are missing the personal **a**.
Write out the ones which need the personal **a** correctly.

a Estoy buscando un autobús. ....

b Llamé mi profesor. ....

c Vi una nube muy grande. ....

d Visitará su abuela. ....

6 Fill in the gaps in these sentences using **por** or **para**.

a Escribí esta tarjeta .... Melissa porque es su cumpleaños.

b El tren .... Madrid va a salir en diez minutos.

c Eduardo pagó treinta euros .... los zapatos.

d Tenemos suficiente dinero .... tres días.

e El viento entró .... la ventana.

Higher

f He perdido mis gafas .... aquí.

g No puede ir a la fiesta .... su trabajo.

h ¿Cuál es la mejor hora de quedar, ... ti?

7 Complete the sentences below by circling the correct conjunction in **bold**.

a Estudian música **e** / **y** inglés.

b ¿Quieres dos **o** / **u** tres huevos?

c Cuesta setenta **o** / **u** ochenta euros.

d Quiero ir de compras **e** / **y** jugar en el parque.

8 Fill in the gaps in these sentences with the most appropriate conjunction.

a Puedes hacerlo .... quieres. **ya que / si / pues**

b Quiero pasear .... está lloviendo. **que / pero / con**

c Arón preparaba la cena .... su novio iba al parque. **o / ya que / para**

d .... debes ir a la cama si estás cansado. **Como / Pues / Que**

e Voy a la playa .... hace sol. **que / porque / para**

f No me gustaría trabajar .... doctor. **como / con / que**

Higher

9 Translate these sentences into **Spanish** using the correct conjunction.

a I can't sleep even though I am tired. ....

b However, the weather was great. ....

c On the other hand, I don't like maths. ....

d My favourite food isn't chicken, but rather fish. ....

e I speak neither English nor Spanish. ....

Adjectives

1 Underline all of the adjectives in the sentences below.

a Las vistas son extraordinarias.

b Vi a una mujer muy vieja.

c Muchas personas vienen a la fiesta.

d Tiene el pelo castaño y largo.

e Leí una historia muy emocionante.

f Poca gente visita el palacio.

g Es un plan perfecto.

h Mi tío dice que la película es divertida.

2 Using the word **pequeño** with the correct endings, translate these phrases into **Spanish**.

a the small mountain

....

b the small house

....

c the small eyes

....

d the small bottles

....

e the small man

....

f the small shoes

....

3 Circle the correct form of the adjectives in **bold** to complete each of these phrases.

a un perro **grande / grandes**

b el gato **contento / contenta**

c tres chicas **bajos / bajas**

d dos asignaturas **fácil / fáciles**

e un modelo **alto / altos**

f dos directores **feliz / felices**

g el examen **difícil / difíciles**

h las flores **bonita / bonitas**

i el caballo **peligroso / peligrosa**

j una camisa **hermoso / hermosa**

4 Translate these sentences into **Spanish** using the adjectives in the box to help.

a Thandiwe is a happy girl. ....

b My teachers are nice. ....

c Football is easy. ....

d She buys three interesting books. ....

e Ben and Adam are young. ....

joven
fácil
simpático
interesante
feliz

5 Translate the English sentences into **Spanish** by putting the words in the right order.

Example Vanessa has few friends. / **tiene pocos Vanessa amigos**

Vanessa tiene pocos amigos.

a The girl eats another omelette. / **tortilla come la otra chica**

....

b Many children play football. / **niños juegan fútbol al muchos**

....

c I liked the first film. / **gustó primera la me película**

....

6 Complete the sentences below by circling the correct form of each adjective.

a Hace **bueno** / **buen** tiempo.

b No había **ninguno** / **ningún** coche.

c Es un **mal** / **malo** profesor.

d **Algún** / **Alguna** gente cree que es una **mal** / **mala** idea.

7 Some adjectives change their meaning depending on where they are in a sentence. Put a tick next to the sentences that have been correctly translated.

a Tengo un jersey nuevo. *I have a newly-made jumper.*

b El perro pobre tiene hambre. *The poor dog is hungry.*

c Ella es una mujer grande. *She's a great woman.*

d Voy a la única fiesta. *I'm going to the only party.*

8 Fill in the gaps in the Spanish sentences with the correct possessive adjectives to match the English sentences.

Possessive adjectives are words like 'mi' and 'tu' ('my' and 'your').

a .... padres son alegres. *My parents are cheerful.*

b Vi a .... amigo en la calle. *I saw your (inf., pl.) friend in the street.*

c .... vecinos se llaman Rita y Pau. *Our neighbours are called Rita and Pau.*

d .... bicicletas son rojas. *Their bicycles are red.*

e ¿Ha visto .... tarjeta? *Have you seen your (form., sing.) card?*

Higher

9 Complete the sentences below by circling the correct form of each adjective.

a Las fotos son **mías** / **vuestros**.

b La televisión es **suyo** / **vuestra**.

c Los billetes son **mío** / **tuyos**.

d Este piso es **nuestro** / **suya**.

e Aquel libro es **mío** / **tuya**.

f Los bolígrafos son **vuestro** / **suyos**.

10 Translate these phrases into **Spanish** using the correct demonstrative adjectives.

Demonstrative adjectives are words like 'este' ('this').

a I live in this street. ....

b I would like those sandwiches. ....

c Do you (inf., sing.) like that castle? ....

H d They are in those boxes over there. ....

11 Fill in the gaps in these sentences with a word from the box. You should use each word **once**.

cada	todos	otro	otra	cada	todas

a Quiero .... fiesta.

b .... persona necesita un libro.

c Me gustan .... sus canciones.

d Lavo mi ropa .... semana.

e Invité a .... mis amigos.

f Necesito .... huevo.

12 Translate these sentences into **Spanish**.

a Mahmood is taller than you. ....

b Jade is as tired as Abel. ....

c English is less easy than Spanish. ....

d My sisters are as funny as me. ....

e Gabriel is younger than Emiko. ....

f The pasta is worse than the rice. ....

Higher

13 Complete these sentences, using the bit in brackets to help you.

a Esta clase es .... del día. (**the least boring**)

b El empresario es .... de mi país. (**the most rich**)

c Manuel es .... de sus amigos. (**the oldest**)

d Ellas son .... profesoras. (**the best**)

Adverbs

1 Make each of these adjectives into an adverb.

a lento .... **d** posible ....

b fácil .... **e** exacto ....

c negativo .... **f** serio ....

2 Translate these sentences into **Spanish**, using the adjective in brackets to help you make the adverb.

a They speak very sadly. (**triste**) ....

b We must leave quickly. (**rápido**) ....

c The level is dangerously low. (**peligroso**) ....

d She sings beautifully. (**bello**) ....

3 Each of these sentences has an error in it. Rewrite each adverb correctly on the dotted line.

a Me gusta mucho cantar. Canto buenamente. ....

b Thomas escribe muy malo. ....

c Jugamos al baloncesto maravillosomente. ....

d Las niñas participan activomente. ....

4 Translate these sentences into **Spanish**.

a The supermarket is very far. ....

b Here one can see a castle. ....

c Many people study there. ....

d I walk to school because it's very near. ....

e There aren't any neighbours upstairs. ....

H **f** You will find the medicine inside the bag. ....

5 Fill in the gaps with the most appropriate adverb chosen from the options.

a Voy a hacer mis deberes más .... **ya / tarde / ahora**

b Me despierto y .... me levanto. **antes / después**

c Mi primo .... ha comido así. **luego / siempre**

d .... es difícil saber la verdad. **Antes / A veces**

e .... estoy seguro. **Antes / Ahora / Temprano**

H **f** .... te vamos a llamar. **Casi / Aún**

6 Translate each of these adverbial phrases into **English**.

a a menudo ....

b a veces ....

c en línea ....

d a pie ....

e al aire libre ....

f al extranjero ....

g de vacaciones ....

h de vez en cuando ....

7 Adverbs can also be used to form comparatives.
Make these sentences make sense by circling one of the words in **bold**.

a Claudia habla más seriamente **que / como** Isaac.

b Kanchana piensa **menos / tan** positivamente que Dani.

c Me encanta trabajar. Trabajo **más / menos** alegremente que mi equipo.

d Mi hijo menor no duerme tan **tranquilamente / tranquila** como su hermano.

e Corro más **rápidamente / lentamente** que mis amigas. ¡No voy a ganar nunca!

f Yo pinto bien, pero ella pinta **mejor / mayor**.

g Él baila **peor / más mal** que sus hermanos.

Higher

8 Translate these sentences into **English**.

a Elisa es la que come menos sanamente. ....

b Ellos son los que celebran más felizmente. ....

c Simran es la que peor actúa. ....

d Lucas es el que mejor cocina. ....

Quantifiers and Intensifiers

1 Cross out the incorrect quantifiers in **bold** to complete these sentences.

a Tengo **demasiado** / **muchos** primos.

b Soy pobre. Tengo **poco** / **poca** dinero.

c Olumide compra **muchos** / **muchas** chaquetas.

d Tienes **demasiados** / **demasiadas** faldas.

e Ahora, Mei viaja **poca** / **poco**.

f Comimos **demasiado** / **poca** queso.

g Mis amigos salen **mucho** / **muchos** al cine.

H h Hay **tanto** / **tanta** ropa que necesitamos organizarla.

i Hiciste **tantos** / **tanto** pasteles que no hay espacio en la cocina.

2 Translate these sentences into **Spanish**.

a English is quite difficult. ....

b I think that pop music is very boring. ....

c Jodie was very ill on Monday. ....

d It's quite an interesting book. ....

e My dog is not very happy today. ....

f Their trousers are quite long. ....

3 Add the suffix -ísimo/a to each adjective to change its meaning. You can use the hint in the brackets to help you, but you may have to change its ending.

a El campo es **really calm**. .... **(tranquilo)**

b Creo que los zapatos son **really big**. .... **(grande)**

c Pienso que ella es **really beautiful**. .... **(bello)**

d El gato es **really slow**. .... **(lento)**

e Las casas nuevas son **really modern**. .... **(moderno)**

Present Tense

1 Write each of these verbs in **Spanish** in their infinitive form.

a to have .... **d** to sing .... **g** to say ....

b to want .... **e** to prefer .... **h** to make ....

c to live .... **f** to think .... **i** to bring ....

2 Fill in the gaps in these sentences with the right form of **visitar** (a regular **-ar** verb).

a Yo .... a mi amigo.

b Tú .... muchas ciudades.

c La mujer .... a su tía.

d Fred y yo .... a nuestros abuelos.

e ¿Vosotros .... a Naomi?

f Esther y Sam .... París.

visitamos
visita
visitáis
visito
visitan
visitas

3 Fill in the table to show **beber** (a regular **-er** verb) in the present tense.

English	Spanish	English	Spanish
I drink		we drink	
you (inf., sing.) drink	*bebes*	you (inf., pl.) drink	
he/she/it drinks		they drink	
you (form., sing.) drink		you (form., pl.) drink	

4 Complete each sentence by circling the correct form of **escribir** (a regular **-ir** verb).

a Sita y Haruki **escribe / escriben** muchas cartas.

b Alexei, ¿**escribes / escribimos** una novela?

c Yo **escribo / escribe** cerca del mar.

d Mi hermana **escribes / escribe** cada día.

e ¿Usted **escribes / escribe / escribís** mucho?

f Adita y yo **escribimos / escriben** letras de canciones.

5 Tom has written these Spanish sentences, but he has made some mistakes with his stem-changing verbs. Write out the sentences correctly.

a Yo penso que él tiene un perro. ....

b Las clases comenzan a las ocho. ....

c Prefero hacer deporte al aire libre. ....

d No duermo bien cuando llove. ....

e Repeten sus errores cada vez. ....

f Reduco mi uso de energía. ....

6 Complete the sentences by filling in the gaps. Watch out for any irregular forms.

a Yo .... mis deberes en la mesa. **haco / hago / hace**

b Nkiru y Jon .... a la tienda. **van / va / vas**

c Tú .... una bicicleta nueva. **ten / tienes / tiene**

d Yo .... al club los martes. **veno / vengo / ven**

e Los viernes, yo .... a Durham. **vo / voy / va**

f Ellos no .... miedo. **tienen / tenen / tenéis**

g Yo te .... uno de mis churros. **doy / da / do**

h Nosotras .... frío. **tenemos / tenéis / tienen**

i Yo .... hablar inglés. **sabo / sé / sabe**

7 Decide whether you need **ser** or **estar** in each of these sentences. Underline your answer.

a ¡Hola! **Soy / Estoy** George.

b No puedo venir a tu fiesta. **Soy / Estoy** de vacaciones.

c No **somos / estamos** de Valencia.

d Hannah **es / está** una persona bastante trabajadora.

e Ethan **es / está** triste porque ha perdido su dinero.

f Tú **eres / estás** más bajo que yo.

g Todas mis primas **son / están** profesoras.

h ¿Por qué **sois / estáis** aquí?

Past Tenses

1 Finish these sentences by adding the correct preterite tense ending to the verb.

a Ishmael viaj.............. mucho.

b Joaquín y yo sal.............. ayer.

c Tú tom.............. la foto.

d El concierto dur.............. una hora.

e Yo abr.............. la puerta.

f Nosotros escrib.............. una historia interesante.

g Vosotros com.............. todo el pan.

h Carl e Irene aprob.............. el examen.

i Mi hermana merec.............. su resultado.

j Erica y Kate beb.............. café.

2 Fill in the gaps by choosing the correct preterite verb.

a Mercedes, ¿tú .... a la piscina? **fue / fuiste / fuisteis**

b Mis primos y yo .... la caja en el coche. **pusisteis / pusieron / pusimos**

c Yo .... mis libros. **traje / trajo / trajiste**

d Vosotras .... al espectáculo. **vinieron / viniste / vinisteis**

3 Match the **Spanish** sentences on the left with their **English** translations on the right.

a Iba a la biblioteca en bicicleta.

b Hacía viento en la ciudad.

c Veía las noticias cada tarde.

d Tocaba la guitarra en el jardín.

e Eras bastante tranquila.

i *He used to watch the news every evening.*

ii *I used to go to the library by bicycle.*

iii *She was playing the guitar in the garden.*

iv *You used to be quite relaxed.*

v *It was windy in the city.*

4 Translate these sentences into **Spanish** using the imperfect form of the verb.

a You (inf., sing.) used to be a teacher. ....

b I used to watch films on Fridays. ....

c He used to sing in the car. ....

d It was raining in the countryside. ....

e She was practising a lot. ....

f There were flowers in the garden. ....

H **g** They used to go to that supermarket. ....

5 Fill in the gaps by choosing between the preterite and imperfect forms.

a Siempre .... en el salón. **descansaste / descansabas**

b El lunes .... al colegio. **fui / iba**

c Ayer, Pedro .... la verdad a su madre. **dijo / decía**

d De niña, Wahiba siempre .... alegre. **fue / era**

e Ayer .... buen tiempo. **hizo / hacía**

f .... feliz el día de mi cumpleaños. **Estuve / Estaba**

H **g** Los jueves .... con sus padres. **quedaron / quedaban**

H **h** .... las compras los fines de semana. **Hicimos / Hacíamos**

6 Translate the following sentences into **Spanish**.

a I went to the park and I lost my glasses. ....

b It was sunny and the children were singing. ....

c When I heard the noise, I was at home. ....

H **d** They were walking when they saw the cat. ....

7 You can use past participles with the verb 'haber' to say what you 'have done'. Write out the past participles for these verbs.

a hablar .... **e** dormir .... **i** decir ....

b pedir .... **f** comprar .... **j** escribir ....

c beber .... **g** perder .... **k** romper ....

d ayudar .... **h** vestir .... H **l** descubrir ....

8 Change these sentences from the present tense into the perfect tense. The first one has been done for you.

Example Estoy en Madrid. *He estado en Madrid.*

a Como un bocadillo de queso. ....

b Lucía termina una historia interesante. ....

c Recibes una carta del banco. ....

d Llegan a casa muy tarde. ....

e Hacemos un viaje a España. ....

The Future, The Conditional and Modal Verbs

1 Match each Spanish sentence on the left with its English translation on the right.

a	Van a estudiar para su examen.	**i**	*You (inf., pl.) are going to close the window.*
b	Voy a pedir dos botellas de agua.	**ii**	*You (inf., sing.) are going to travel this summer.*
c	Vas a viajar este verano.	**iii**	*They are going to study for their exam.*
d	Vamos a salir mañana.	**iv**	*We are going to go out tomorrow.*
e	Vais a cerrar la ventana.	**v**	*I am going to ask for two bottles of water.*

2 Using the present tense of **ir**, fill in the gaps to create sentences in the immediate future tense.

a (Nosotros) .... a hacer las compras esta tarde.

b (Tú) .... a casarte con José.

c (Yo) .... a pagar la cuenta.

d (Ella) .... a beber el té.

e (Ellos) .... a estar de vacaciones desde mañana.

3 Fill in thc gaps with the correct proper future tense form of the verbs given in brackets.

a Noelia te .... (**to bring**) el juego.

b El sábado tú .... (**to sing**) la canción maravillosa que escribiste.

c Escucha bien porque yo .... (**to repeat**) la pregunta solo una vez.

d Tu primo no .... (**to have**) mucho tiempo para verte.

H **e** Mis amigos y yo .... (**to visit**) el museo de historia natural.

H **f** Patricia y Mauricio .... (**to come**) con nosotros en la piscina mañana.

4 Translate these sentences into **Spanish**.

a She will call me tomorrow night. ....

b I will put the pens on the table. ....

c There will be lots of people in the café. ....

H **d** We will go out next week. ....

H **e** Will you (inf., pl.) say something to your friends? ....

5 Complete these sentences by writing the verbs in brackets in the correct form of the conditional.

a Julieta .... (**viajar**) por el mundo en su barco.

b Yo .... (**hacer**) los vestidos para el próximo espectáculo.

c Con todo ese dinero, tú .... (**poder**) comprar una isla.

Higher

d Entonces, ¿nunca .... (**dar**) regalos a vuestros amigos?

e Mis padres .... (**saber**) cómo resolver el problema.

f Femi .... (**querer**) ir a otro restaurante para la cena.

6 Complete these sentences by translating the bits in brackets into **Spanish**.

a Aunque no tiene hambre, ... (*he would eat*)

b Sé que me .... con esto. (*you (inf., sing.) would help*)

c .... un recuerdo, pero no tengo dinero. (*I would buy*)

Higher

d .... dormir aquí por esta noche. (*We should*)

e .... su casa para vivir en otro lugar. (*They would sell*)

f .... alquilar un coche después de llegar. (*You (form., pl.) could*)

7 Choose the **modal verb** from the right and put it in the correct present tense form to fill in the gaps.

a Yo no .... jugar al fútbol porque lo odio. **interesar / querer / disfrutar**

b Lo siento, pero no .... *(nosotros)* venir. **invitar / reunirse / poder**

c .... levantarte ahora para ir al colegio. **deber / tener / decidir**

d Mi hermano todavía no .... cocinar. **conocer / saber / aprender**

e Los alumnos .... prepararse para el examen. **ir a / pensar en / tener que**

8 Translate these sentences into **English**.

a Me gustaría vivir en un barrio más tranquilo.

....

b Quisiera reservar una habitación, por favor.

....

c Busca vuelos porque le gustaría viajar.

....

Reflexives, '-ing' Verbs, Negatives and Impersonal Verbs

1 Fill in the correct reflexive pronoun in each of the sentences below.

a .... quedo en un hotel.

b .... pones enfadado fácilmente.

c .... lleva bien con su familia.

d .... pierde en la ciudad.

H

e .... vestimos rápidamente.

f .... acostáis muy tarde normalmente.

2 Put these verbs into the correct present tense form.

a llamarse (tú) ....

b dormirse (yo) ....

c levantarse (ella) ....

Higher

d despertarse (nosotros) ....

e sentirse (vosotros) ....

f cambiarse (ustedes) ....

3 Fill in the gaps in these sentences with the correct option from the brackets.

a Mañana voy a .... (**levantarme** / **me levantar**) a las ocho y media.

b Si .... (**preparas te** / **te preparas**) bien, tendrás éxito en el examen.

c Mi novio está enfadado porque no puede .... (**se duerme** / **dormirse**).

d Ya han llegado y ahora .... (**me debo vestir** / **debome vestir**) rápidamente.

4 Write the present participle (the '-ing' form) for each of these verbs.

a correr ....

b mandar ....

c caer ....

d cerrar ....

e seguir ....

f dormir ....

g encontrar ....

h oír ....

5 Complete these sentences by translating the bits in brackets into **Spanish** using the imperfect continuous.

a .... mucho para terminar el proyecto. (*She was working*)

b .... una serie hasta las ocho de la tarde. (*I was watching*)

c Me .... algo, pero no lo oí. (*You (inf., sing.) were saying*)

d Cuando vi a Marco, ... en la biblioteca. (*He was reading*)

Higher

6 Translate these sentences into **English**.

a Sigo tomando el desayuno. ....

b Nina lleva seis horas pintando. ....

c Acabamos de ganar la competición. ....

d Viven aquí desde hace dos años. ....

7 Translate these sentences into **Spanish** by putting the words in the right order.

Example Nothing happens here on Sundays. / **pasa los aquí domingos nada**

Nada pasa aquí los domingos.

a No, I don't want to clean today. / **quiero no limpiar no hoy**

....

b Nobody is in the kitchen. / **está cocina la nadie en**

....

c They never watch films in the cinema. / **películas en ven el nunca cine las**

....

Higher

8 Translate these sentences into **Spanish**.

a Jiahao no longer teaches science. ....

b I eat neither meat nor fish. ....

c He does not speak to us either. ....

9 Put the missing impersonal verb into the Spanish sentences to match the English translation.

a .... terminar el libro ahora. — *You (general) need to finish the book now.*

b .... bonitas flores en el jardín. — *There are pretty flowers in the garden.*

c .... pasear por el parque. — *One can go for a walk through the park.*

d .... ir a la caja para pagar. — *You (general) must go to the till to pay.*

H

e .... hablar con él en persona. — *It's worth speaking with him in person.*

f .... encontrar una solución. — *It's necessary to find a solution.*

The Passive, Subjunctive and Imperative

Higher

1 Underline the passive voice used in these sentences. Careful — not all of them contain the passive.

a El autobús salió a las tres y cuarto.

b La compañía fue creada por mi abuela.

c La fábrica produce mucho ruido.

d El baño será pintado por sus hermanos.

e La exposición fue vista por muchos turistas.

f Los bosques son protegidos por la ley.

g La pareja ha viajado por el mundo.

h El paciente fue visitado por el médico.

i Se lavaron las manos antes de comer.

j Ayer se despertó tarde por accidente.

Higher

2 Write the endings of these past participles. Make sure they agree with the subject.

a El premio fue ganad........ por el equipo local.

b Los libros son escrit........ por un autor famoso.

c La fuente fue construid........ por los españoles.

d Las tapas fueron comid........ por la niña.

e La clase será enseñad........ por mi padre.

f El partido es elegid........ por la gente.

Higher

3 Match these Spanish sentences on the left with their English translations on the right.

a ¿Se venden gafas de sol aquí?

b Se juega al baloncesto en el parque.

c Los billetes se compran en línea.

d ¿Las puertas se van a abrir pronto?

e Se sirve el pan con la cena.

i *Tickets are bought online.*

ii *Are the doors going to open soon?*

iii *The bread is served with dinner.*

iv *Are sunglasses sold here?*

v *Basketball is played in the park.*

Higher

4 Give the present subjunctive forms of these verbs, matching the person given.

a venir — ella ....

b ser — tú ....

c hacer — él ....

d ir — tú ....

e tener — yo ....

f ir — usted ....

Higher

5 Put the verbs in brackets into the correct form of the present subjunctive or present indicative to fill in the gaps in these sentences.

a Creemos que Nico .... las entradas. (**tener**)

b Viviré en el extranjero cuando .... mayor. (**ser**)

c Es necesario que tú .... conmigo. (**venir**)

d Es verdad que Isidora .... a la plaza para tomar un café. (**ir**)

e Mis profesores quieren que yo .... mis deberes. (**hacer**)

6 Write out the following verbs as singular informal commands.

a cantar ....

b abrir ....

c hacer ....

d ser ....

e dar ....

f aprender ....

g decir ....

h mirar ....

i venir ....

j hablar ....

k tener ....

l salir ....

7 Choose the correct verb from the box, then write it as a singular informal command to fill in the gaps.

a ¡ .... tus deberes!

b ¡ .... a tu habitación ahora!

c ¡ .... la ropa sucia aquí!

d ¡ .... en el jardín, no en la casa!

poner
terminar
ir
jugar

8 Translate these imperatives into **Spanish**. The word in brackets tells you what 'it' is referring to.

a Call him! ....

b Tell me! ....

c Wash it! (*the car*) ....

d Eat it! (*the burger*) ....

Higher

9 Write the verbs in brackets as plural informal commands.

a .... (**tomar**) la primera calle a la derecha para llegar al banco.

b .... (**servir**) azúcar y leche con su té.

c ¡ .... (**dejar**) de discutir, por favor!

d ¡ .... (**escoger**) la opción correcta para ganar!

e .... (**subir**) a la segunda planta ahora.

Answers

The answers to the translation questions are sample answers only, just to give you an idea of one way to translate them. There may be different ways to translate these sentences that are also correct.

For dictation and translation questions, this symbol (|) shows where to divide the marks. There is 1 mark awarded for the first part of the text, and 1 mark awarded for the second.

Section One — General Stuff

Pages 2-3: Numbers, Times, Days and Dates

1) a) Intento estar activo | cada día.
   b) Cada mañana, camino | treinta minutos.
   c) Mi novia baila | dos veces a la semana.
   d) En el verano, preferimos | montar en nuestras bicicletas.
   e) El año pasado, corrí | cincuenta kilómetros en una competición.
2) a) on the second floor
   b) It's easier to listen to the teacher.
3) a) December
   b) August
   c) from midday
   d) his house
   e) the park
4) a) B, E and F
   b) i) 132 euros
      ii) so he won't have as far to travel (the morning of the flight)
      iii) midday / 12:00

Pages 4-5: Questions and Being Polite

1) a) Omar
   b) Hugo
   c) Nadia
   d) Omar
   e) Nadia
   f) Hugo
2) Here are some examples of sentences you could have written:
   Hay un grupo de estudiantes.
   Están en una clase con la profesora.
   Varios estudiantes tienen una pregunta.
   La profesora les responde.
3) B, D and F
4) a) to ask her some questions
   b) (he has taken) a photo for his ID card
   c) if he needs to wear a suit
   d) if colleagues share cars (to get to work)
   e) Any one from:
      He has just moved to the area.
      He doesn't know anyone.
      He would like to get to know his colleagues well.

Pages 6-7: Opinions

2) a) (because it has very) beautiful gardens
   b) flamenco shows
   c) (it is) incredible
3) a) water
   b) coffee
   c) fish
   d) chocolate
4) a) interesting worlds / characters that live in interesting worlds
   b) publish a novel
   c) she enjoys it / to sing them in her band
   d) Any one from:
      She is nervous.
      (it will be) an exciting experience
      She will never forget it.

Section Two — Identity and Relationships with Others

Pages 8-9: About Yourself and My Family & Friends

1) a) I spend a lot of time with my family.
   b) I get on very well with my sister.
   c) She is called Luisa and she has green eyes.
   d) Last Sunday we went to a museum together.
   e) Today we are visiting our cousin on the coast for his birthday.
2) a) C b) A c) B
3) a) Mi <u>hermana</u> <u>mayor</u> está <u>embarazada</u>.
   b) Estoy <u>emocionado</u> de <u>conocer</u> a mi <u>sobrino</u>.
   c) Me llevo bien con | mi hermano gemelo.
   d) Somos los menores | en nuestra familia.
   e) Nacimos en México | hace quince años.
   f) Estoy orgulloso de | mi identidad latina.

Pages 10-11: Describing People and Relationships

1) A, C and D
4) a) green
   b) music
   c) comedies
5) When I was little, | I was the shortest in my class. | I am no longer short, | but rather tall. | I also have long dark hair | that I wear in a headscarf. | Various artistic figures have had | a huge influence on my style. | Art and fashion have always helped me | to express myself without fear.

Pages 12-13: Role Models and Celebrations

1) Here are some examples of sentences you could have written:
   Hay un hombre y un chico.
   Están en un estadio.
   El chico está feliz.
   El hombre lleva ropa de deporte.
2) a) (every) New Year's Eve
   b) His sister is getting married.
   c) He is ill.
3) a) B b) A c) B d) C

Section Three — Healthy Living

Pages 14-15: Food

1) Here are some examples of sentences you could have written:
   Hay una familia de cuatro personas.
   Son dos chicos y sus padres.
   Están en la cocina.
   Preparan pasta para la cena.
2) a) B
   b) A
   c) B
3) a) meat
   b) dessert
   c) coffee
4) B, C and E

Pages 16-17: Physical & Mental Wellbeing and Illnesses & Treatments

2) B, D and E
3) a) B
   b) C
   c) B
   d) A

Section Four — Free-time Activities

Pages 18-19: Music, Cinema and TV

1) a) walking
   b) in class
   c) rock
2) A, D and F
3) Me encanta ver la televisión | porque es muy relajante. | Veía los documentales de naturaleza después del colegio | pero ahora prefiero ver las noticias o una serie. | Para mí, las películas | son bastante difíciles de ver. | Duran mucho más tiempo que | los programas de televisión. | Empezaré a ver la nueva temporada de | mi drama favorito actual esta noche.
4) a) i) B ii) C iii) B iv) A
   b) A

Pages 20-21: Sports, Going Out and Other Hobbies

1) a) Cris b) Lin c) Cris d) Ana e) Lin f) Ana
2) a) A b) C c) A
4) I have been doing sports | for nine years. | Swimming is my passion and | I usually practise it three times a week. | Last season my friend and I participated in a competition | and my friend won a prize. | When I do my exams | I will have less time to do sport. | However, after finishing them | I will return to competitions.

Themes 1 and 2 — Mixed Practice

Pages 22-25: Mixed Practice — Foundation

1) a) i) C ii) B
   b) C
3) Here are some examples of sentences you could have written:
   Hay dos personas.
   Están en la calle.
   Corren juntos.
   Llevan ropa deportiva.
4) B, C and F
5) a) Me encanta <u>leer</u> las <u>revistas</u>.
   b) Escribir historias | es muy interesante.
6) a) This morning, I need | to go to the hospital.
   b) I have an appointment | because my throat hurts.
   c) I already take tablets | and they are quite strong.
   d) The doctors are kind | and they help me a lot.
   e) Last week, my sister was | also very sick.
7) A, D and F

Pages 26-27: Mixed Practice — Both Tiers

1) a) A b) B c) A
2) a) in the swimming pool b) (his) back
4) a) stepbrother
   b) sister
   c) city
   d) funny
   e) hard-working

Pages 28-31: Mixed Practice — Higher

2) a) i) a lack of exercise / little knowledge about healthy food
   ii) the government
   b) B
3) a) C, D and F
   b) i) He's too old for it.
   ii) They came to see him (at home).
   iii) The water reduces pressure on his leg.
   iv) being more active
4) Acabo de organizar una fiesta | para el doce de diciembre. | Empieza a las siete menos cuarto | y va a durar cuatro horas. | Treinta y ocho personas asistirán al evento, | incluso toda mi familia. | Fui a otra celebración recientemente | y fue muy aburrida. | Sin embargo, | me gustó mucho la comida.
6) My passion is cooking | since it is an important part of Mexican culture. | My mother hates junk food, | so she always prepares fresh dishes. | Also, she taught my brothers and me to cook | when we were little. | I used to be vegan, but I am not anymore | because it was difficult to follow that diet. | I would love | to open a vegetarian restaurant.
7) a) Karima is shorter. / Karima has lighter hair.
   b) their personalities
   c) singing (in a band)
   d) She always has (someone for) company.
   e) (Many) people want to compare them.

Section Five — Places in Town

Pages 32-33: Where You Live and At Home

1) Here are some examples of sentences you could have written:
   Hay una chica.
   Está limpiando una mesa.
   Escucha música.
   Lleva una camiseta blanca.
2) a) B
   b) A
   c) C
3) a) **One detail about his mornings**
   gets up at seven / gets dressed first
   When he goes to bed
   quarter past ten
   b) **One thing she likes doing to help**
   preparing dinner
   What she will do at the weekend
   go on a trip (with her family)

Pages 34-35: The Local Area

1) a) Mi <u>ciudad</u> tiene <u>muchos</u> bares.
   b) Me gusta <u>visitar</u> el <u>observatorio</u>.
   c) La <u>plaza</u> principal es <u>gigante</u>.
   d) Siempre hay algo que hacer.
   e) Mañana quiero ir al mercado.
3) a) A
   b) C
   c) C
4) a) i) new activities at the gym / a theatre opened
   ii) a discount for a (theatre) show
   b) B

Pages 36-37: Shopping, Directions and Weather

2) Hoy hace sol y calor. | La semana pasada, hizo viento | y llovió durante tres días. | Lo peor fue que | no pude ir al parque | con mis amigos. | Sin embargo, según las noticias, | no habrá más lluvia esta semana. | Por lo tanto, podré pasar | mucho tiempo al aire libre.
4) a) i) C
   ii) B
   b) i) behind the (sports) centre
   ii) (because) there was lots of snow

Section Six — Environmental and Social Issues

Pages 38-39: Environmental Problems, Effects and Protection

1) a) I like | riding a bike.
   b) It is better for the environment | than travelling by car.
   c) Yesterday I took the bus to go to school | and it was very quick.
   d) Public transport protects the planet, | since it uses less energy.
2) a) sun
   b) snow
   c) forests
   d) green spaces
4) Here are some examples of sentences you could have written:
   Hay tres personas.
   Están en una playa.
   Hace viento.
   Recogen plástico en bolsas.
5) B, D and F

Pages 40-41: Equality and Social Issues

1) a) i) C   ii) A
   b) A
2) B, D and E
4) Me encanta nuestro mundo multicultural, | pero desafortunadamente no es igual. | La igualdad es un tema | que me importa mucho. | Un artículo reciente dijo que la mayoría de la gente | conoce a una víctima de la discriminación. | Para mí, es necesario enseñar a todos | cómo mejorar la sociedad y hacerla igual. | Tenemos más poder | si trabajamos juntos.

Section Seven — Social Media and Technology

Pages 42-43: Technology, The Internet and Streaming

2) a) She finds information for her homework.
   b) presents
   c) Someone got into her online shopping account.
   d) make sure that each password is secure
4) a) (our) lifestyles have changed (enormously)
   b) reduce fear of technology
   c) people older than eighteen
   d) Any one from:
      doing web searches / finding information
      shopping online
      sending and receiving emails
   e) a virtual qualification

Pages 44-45: Social Media

2) a) (through) direct messages
   b) photos
   c) stop people writing them
3) a) accounts
   b) messages
   c) healthy
4) a) **Advantage**: (It's) easy to organise parties with friends.
      Disadvantage: (It's) irritating to keep up with contacts.
   b) **Advantage**: She can find interesting / beautiful places.
      Disadvantage: Some people don't talk much in real life anymore.

Themes 3 and 4 — Mixed Practice

Pages 46-49: Mixed Practice — Foundation

1) a) Me gusta usar | los servicios de streaming.
   b) Son útiles | para bajar música.
   c) Comparto canciones | en las redes sociales.
   d) También hago contenido | con mis amigos en línea.
   e) El mes pasado | subimos un vídeo divertido.
3) B, C and F
4) a) B   b) C   c) A   d) C
6) a) Quiero hacer una diferencia | en el mundo.
   b) El hambre es un problema | en mi barrio.
   c) Voy a un club de jóvenes | para ayudar a otros.
   d) Ayer cocinamos comidas | para nuestra comunidad.
7) a) **One improvement in her town**
      Putting benches in parks /
      Putting sports equipment in parks
      One reason
      More to do when it's sunny /
      People will enjoy being outdoors more
   b) **One improvement in his town**
      Improved the roads in the centre /
      Cleaned the main square
      One reason
      Makes it a safer area /
      Makes it prettier
   c) **One improvement in her town**
      Opened a public garden /
      Put more nature outside buildings
      One reason
      Made a new space for events /
      Made the town greener

Pages 50-51: Mixed Practice — Both Tiers

1) a) fast
   b) broken
   c) mobile phone
   d) series
   e) stream
3) a) i) B   ii) A   iii) B   iv) C
   b) A

Pages 52-55: Mixed Practice — Higher

1) a) **Advantage:** (It's) cheaper than living alone.
      Disadvantage: Some people don't do any chores.
   b) **Advantage:** (They) share the responsibility for cooking. / (They both) save money.
      Disadvantage: His cousin has friends over until late (at night).
   c) **Advantage:** He has someone to talk to (when he comes home).
      Disadvantage: There isn't enough space (for everyone).
2) Colgué un nuevo vídeo en Internet | la semana pasada. | Se trataba de | la seguridad en las redes sociales. | Para mí, estas redes son prácticas | para comunicarme con mis amigos. | Sin embargo, hay peligros | y es importante enseñar a la gente cómo evitarlos. | El vídeo creó una discusión interesante | entre mis seguidores.
4) a) i) in a city / in the south (of the country)
      ii) an enormous kitchen / a library full of (old/antique) books
   b) C
5) a) B, C and F
   b) i) It has increased in the last 5 years.
      ii) shop owners
      iii) They're trying to take legal action against the groups.
7) a) rubbish on beaches
   b) serious damage to animal species
   c) (to) keep natural spaces clean
   d) (they will) spend more money on public transport

Section Eight — School

Pages 56-57: School Subjects and School Life

1) i) English
   ii) The sports equipment is old. / The field is too small.
3) I have been attending | my current high school for two years. | My last one was marvellous | and I loved studying there. | Therefore, it was hard | to change schools and come here. | Now I enjoy my classes | and I'm still making friends with my classmates. | Also, we study several languages, | which really interests me.
5) a) El <u>gimnasio</u> en mi <u>colegio</u> | es <u>estupendo</u>.
   b) Encuentro las ciencias | muy prácticas.
   c) El <u>plazo</u> para <u>entregar</u> | el <u>ensayo</u> es estricto.
   d) Soy consciente de | mi comportamiento en clase.

Pages 58-59: School Pressures and Difficulties

1) a) i) C
      ii) B
   b) C
2) B, C and F
4) a) i) talk to someone (about your feelings)
      ii) you can share ideas
   b) B

Section Nine — Future Opportunities

Pages 60-61: Education Post-16 and Career Choices & Ambitions

2) a) You don't need a degree. / You would receive training.
   b) They can be long. / It's sometimes necessary to work at night.
   c) You could help your community.
4) a) B & C
   b) i) singing in public made her nervous
      ii) change schools / go to a special school
      iii) (it will be) judged by experts

Section Ten — Travel and Tourism

Pages 62-63: Where to Go and Accommodation & Travel

1) a) Voy a España | cada verano.
   b) Mi familia coge | el avión.
   c) Visitamos pueblos tranquilos | cerca de la costa.
   d) Me encanta pasar tiempo | al aire libre.
   e) En nuestro último viaje | mi tía alquiló un coche.
3) a) C b) B c) A

Pages 64-65: Tourist Attractions

1) a) **One detail about where she lives**
      they have seven fairs / they celebrate many traditions
      One activity she likes
      preparing food / participating in dances
   b) **One place he likes to be on festival days**
      in the square / on the beach
      What he will celebrate elsewhere
      Carnival
2) a) palace
   b) castle
   c) boat ride
   d) food
   e) maps
4) a) B b) A c) B d) C

Themes 5 and 6 — Mixed Practice

Pages 66-68: Mixed Practice — Foundation

1) a) Lola
   b) Raúl
   c) Lola
   d) Iván
   e) Raúl
   f) Iván
3) B, C and E
4) a) Voy a | una escuela internacional.
   b) Hay sólo | trescientos alumnos.
   c) Disfruto de mis clases | porque son pequeñas.
   d) La semana pasada tuve | muchos deberes de ciencias.
   e) Si saco buenas notas, | puedo ir a la universidad.
5) a) B
   b) C
   c) B
   d) A

Pages 69-72: Mixed Practice — Both Tiers

2) a) A b) C c) A
3) A, C and F
4) a) i) C ii) B
   b) i) several historical sites
      ii) tourists
5) a) B b) C c) B
6) a) **likes** — the (incredible) view
      dislikes — (that) the bed is uncomfortable / (that) the bed hurts his back
   b) **likes** — the hotel's food
      dislikes — (that) the pool is very small
7) a) i) C ii) B iii) C iv) A
   b) A

Pages 73-75: Mixed Practice — Higher

1) After my exams, | I would like to get some work experience. | I have already applied for positions | at three companies in my region. | Yesterday I had a phone interview | with the director of one of these companies. | I think I responded well to her questions | and I feel very optimistic about receiving an offer. | Working there would be | an excellent opportunity.
4) a) do something practical
   b) go to university
   c) scientist
   d) salary, happiness
5) Cuando voy al extranjero | me encanta volar. | Los aviones son la manera más rápida de viajar | y las vistas son increíbles. | Disfruto de todos los tipos de transporte, | salvo los barcos. | Suelen hacerme sentir enfermo | y odio el olor de sal. | Vale la pena probar experiencias de viaje diferentes | porque todas son únicas.
6) a) the countryside
   b) go bike riding through the mountains / walk through forests
   c) fish with rice
   d) They were too tired.
   e) The weather might affect her train.

Section Eleven — Nouns, Articles and Linking Words

Pages 76-77: Nouns and Articles

1) a) Odio la historia y el inglés.
   b) Mi hermano compró unos zapatos nuevos.
   c) Los deberes son siempre difíciles.
   d) Tuviste tres bolígrafos rojos.
   e) Voy a visitar a mi abuelo.
   f) Me dio un regalo grande.
   g) Me gustan los gatos y los perros.
   h) Cada viernes sólo como bocadillos.
   i) Preferiría ir a la costa que ir al campo.
   j) Mis padres conocen a mis amigos.
2) a) m b) f c) m d) m e) m f) f g) f h) m
   i) m j) m k) f l) f m) f n) m o) f p) f
3) a) las verduras
   b) los sábados
   c) las veces
   d) los meses
   e) los estadios
   f) los jardines
   g) las edades
   h) las mujeres
   i) los terrores
   j) las actrices
   k) las voces
   l) los jueves
   m) los exámenes
   n) las camisas
   o) los aviones
4) a) días b) animales c) puertas d) flores e) profesores
5) a) Las b) El c) las d) Los e) el
6) a) Odio correr porque es duro.
   b) Aprendemos las matemáticas.
   c) Los mexicanos preparan comida maravillosa.
   d) La positividad es importante.
7) a) unos, una, un
   b) un, una
   c) un, unas
8) a) Le gustan los huevos y las patatas fritas.
   b) En el futuro, quiere ser artista.
   c) La señora García es mi profesora.
   d) No tengo ordenador.
   e) Lo mejor es que son amigos.

Pages 78-79: Pronouns

1) a) Yo tengo un perro y tú tienes un gato.
   b) Vosotros podéis ir al concierto.
   c) Ella es profesora y él es cantante.
   d) Nosotros estamos aquí, pero ellos están allí.
   e) Ustedes pueden salir ahora.
   f) Usted invitó a Lin a la fiesta.
2) a) lo b) la c) las d) los
3) a) Me dio el libro.
   b) Le envié una carta.
   c) Te llamé ayer.
   d) Les dijimos la verdad.
4) a) mí b) contigo c) ti, él
5) a) algo
   b) todo
   c) alguien
   d) algunos/as
   e) ninguno/a
   f) todos/as
6) a) ¿Quién te llamó?
   b) ¿Qué vamos a hacer?
   c) ¿Cuál preferís?
   d) ¿Cuánto cuesta esto?
   e) ¿De dónde vinieron?
7) a) el que
   b) lo que
   c) que
   d) del cual
   e) la cual
8) a) This doesn't interest me much.
   b) Why did you say that to your cousin?
   c) We don't know what to do with that.
9) a) La mía es azul.
   b) Los tuyos son divertidos.
   c) El suyo es bastante pequeño.
   d) Las nuestras son enormes.

Pages 80-81: Prepositions and Conjunctions

1) a) en b) sobre c) de d) a e) hasta
2) a) iii b) i c) ii d) iv
3) a) entre
   b) desde
   c) durante
   d) salvo
   e) hacia
   f) dentro de
4) a) I like to run in order to be fit.
   b) They leave without taking their mobile phones.
   c) I am going to the concert after having dinner.
5) a) Correct
   b) Llamé a mi profesor.
   c) Correct
   d) Visitará a su abuela.
6) a) para
   b) para
   c) por
   d) para
   e) por
   f) por
   g) por
   h) para
7) a) e b) o c) u d) y
8) a) si b) pero c) ya que d) Pues e) porque f) como
9) a) No puedo dormir aunque estoy cansado.
   b) Sin embargo, el tiempo era genial.
   c) En cambio, no me gustan las matemáticas.
   d) Mi comida favorita no es pollo, sino pescado.
   e) No hablo ni inglés ni español.

Section Twelve — Adjectives and Adverbs

Pages 82-84: Adjectives

1) a) extraordinarias
   b) vieja
   c) Muchas
   d) castaño, largo
   e) emocionante
   f) Poca
   g) perfecto
   h) divertida
2) a) la montaña pequeña
   b) la casa pequeña
   c) los ojos pequeños
   d) las botellas pequeñas
   e) el hombre pequeño
   f) los zapatos pequeños
3) a) grande
   b) contento
   c) bajas
   d) fáciles
   e) alto
   f) felices
   g) difícil
   h) bonitas
   i) peligroso
   j) hermosa
4) a) Thandiwe es una niña feliz.
   b) Mis profesores son simpáticos.
   c) El fútbol es fácil.
   d) Compra tres libros interesantes.
   e) Ben y Adam son jóvenes.
5) a) La chica come otra tortilla.
   b) Muchos niños juegan al fútbol.
   c) Me gustó la primera película.
6) a) buen
   b) ningún
   c) mal
   d) Alguna, mala
7) a) Correct
   b) Incorrect
   c) Incorrect
   d) Correct
8) a) Mis
   b) vuestro
   c) Nuestros
   d) Sus
   e) su
9) a) mías
   b) vuestra
   c) tuyos
   d) nuestro
   e) mío
   f) suyos
10) a) Vivo en esta calle.
    b) Quisiera esos bocadillos.
    c) ¿Te gusta ese castillo?
    d) Están en aquellas cajas.
11) a) otra
    b) Cada
    c) todas
    d) cada
    e) todos
    f) otro
12) a) Mahmood es más alto que tú.
    b) Jade está tan cansado como Abel.
    c) El inglés es menos fácil que el español.
    d) Mis hermanas son tan divertidas como yo.
    e) Gabriel es menor que Emiko.
    f) La pasta es peor que el arroz.
13) a) la menos aburrida
    b) el más rico
    c) el mayor
    d) las mejores

Pages 85-86: Adverbs

1) a) lentamente
   b) fácilmente
   c) negativamente
   d) posiblemente
   e) exactamente
   f) seriamente
2) a) Hablan muy tristemente.
   b) Tenemos que salir rápidamente.
   c) El nivel es peligrosamente bajo.
   d) Canta bellamente.
3) a) bien
   b) mal
   c) maravillosamente
   d) activamente
4) a) El supermercado está muy lejos.
   b) Aquí se puede ver un castillo.
   c) Mucha gente estudia allí.
   d) Camino al colegio porque está muy cerca.
   e) No hay ningunos vecinos arriba.
   f) Encontrarás la medicina dentro de la bolsa.
5) a) tarde
   b) después
   c) siempre
   d) A veces
   e) Ahora
   f) Aún
6) a) often
   b) sometimes
   c) online
   d) on foot
   e) outdoors
   f) abroad
   g) on holiday
   h) from time to time
7) a) que
   b) menos
   c) más
   d) tranquilamente
   e) lentamente
   f) mejor
   g) peor
8) a) Elisa is the one who eats the least healthily.
   b) They're the ones who celebrate the most happily.
   c) Simran is the one who acts the worst.
   d) Lucas is the one who cooks the best.

Page 87: Quantifiers and Intensifiers

1) a) muchos
   b) poco
   c) muchas
   d) demasiadas
   e) poco
   f) demasiado
   g) mucho
   h) tanta
   i) tantos
2) a) El inglés es bastante difícil.
   b) Creo que la música pop es muy aburrida.
   c) Jodie estaba muy enferma el lunes.
   d) Es un libro bastante interesante.
   e) Mi perro no está muy feliz hoy.
   f) Sus pantalones son bastante largos.
3) a) tranquilísimo
   b) grandísimos
   c) bellísima
   d) lentísimo
   e) modernísimas

Section Thirteen — Verbs and Tenses

Pages 88-89: Present Tense

1) a) tener
   b) querer
   c) vivir
   d) cantar
   e) preferir
   f) pensar
   g) decir
   h) hacer
   i) traer
2) a) visito
   b) visitas
   c) visita
   d) visitamos
   e) visitáis
   f) visitan
3)

English	Spanish	English	Spanish
I drink	bebo	we drink	bebemos
you (inf., sing.) drink	*bebes*	you (inf., pl.) drink	bebéis
he/she/it drinks	bebe	they drink	beben
you (form., sing.) drink	bebe	you (form., pl.) drink	beben

4) a) escriben
   b) escribes
   c) escribo
   d) escribe
   e) escribe
   f) escribimos
5) a) Yo pienso que él tiene un perro.
   b) Las clases comienzan a las ocho.
   c) Prefiero hacer deporte al aire libre.
   d) No duermo bien cuando llueve.
   e) Repiten sus errores cada vez.
   f) Reduzco mi uso de energía.

6) a) hago
b) van
c) tienes
d) vengo
e) voy
f) tienen
g) doy
h) tenemos
i) sé

7) a) Soy
b) Estoy
c) somos
d) es
e) está
f) eres
g) son
h) estáis

7) a) hablado
b) pedido
c) bebido
d) ayudado
e) dormido
f) comprado
g) perdido
h) vestido
i) dicho
j) escrito
k) roto
l) descubierto

8) a) He comido un bocadillo de queso.
b) Lucía ha terminado una historia interesante.
c) Has recibido una carta del banco.
d) Han llegado a casa muy tarde.
e) Hemos hecho un viaje a España.

Pages 90-91: Past Tenses

1) a) viajó
b) salimos
c) tomaste
d) duró
e) abrí
f) escribimos
g) comisteis
h) aprobaron
i) mereció
j) bebieron

2) a) fuiste
b) pusimos
c) traje
d) vinisteis

3) a) ii
b) v
c) i
d) iii
e) iv

4) a) Eras profesor(a).
b) Veía películas los viernes.
c) Cantaba en el coche.
d) Llovía en el campo.
e) Practicaba mucho.
f) Había flores en el jardín.
g) Iban a ese supermercado.

5) a) descansabas
b) fui
c) dijo
d) era
e) hizo
f) Estaba
g) quedaban
h) Hacíamos

6) a) Fui al parque y perdí mis gafas.
b) Hacía sol y los niños cantaban.
c) Cuando oí el ruido, estaba en casa.
d) Andaban cuando vieron el gato.

Pages 92-93: The Future, The Conditional and Modal Verbs

1) a) iii
b) v
c) ii
d) iv
e) i

2) a) Vamos
b) Vas
c) Voy
d) Va
e) Van

3) a) traerá
b) cantarás
c) repetiré
d) tendrá
e) visitaremos
f) vendrán

4) a) Me llamará mañana por la noche.
b) Pondré los bolígrafos sobre la mesa.
c) Habrá muchas personas en el café.
d) Saldremos la próxima semana.
e) ¿Diréis algo a vuestros amigos?

5) a) viajaría
b) haría
c) podrías
d) daríais
e) sabrían
f) querría

6) a) comería
b) ayudarías
c) Compraría
d) Deberíamos
e) Venderían
f) Podrían

7) a) quiero
b) podemos
c) Debes
d) sabe
e) tienen que

8) a) I would like to live in a calmer neighbourhood.
b) I would like to reserve a room, please.
c) He is looking for flights because he would like to travel.

Pages 94-95: Reflexives, '-ing' Verbs, Negatives and Impersonal Verbs

1) a) me
   b) te
   c) se
   d) se
   e) nos
   f) os
2) a) te llamas
   b) me duermo
   c) se levanta
   d) nos despertamos
   e) os sentís
   f) se cambian
3) a) levantarme
   b) te preparas
   c) dormirse
   d) me debo vestir
4) a) corriendo
   b) mandando
   c) cayendo
   d) cerrando
   e) siguiendo
   f) durmiendo
   g) encontrando
   h) oyendo
5) a) Estaba trabajando
   b) Estaba viendo
   c) estabas diciendo
   d) estaba leyendo
6) a) I am still eating breakfast.
   b) Nina has been painting for six hours.
   c) We have just won the competition.
   d) They have been living here for two years.
7) a) No, no quiero limpiar hoy.
   b) Nadie está en la cocina.
   c) Nunca ven las películas en el cine.
8) a) Jiahao ya no enseña las ciencias.
   b) No como ni carne ni pescado.
   c) No nos habla tampoco.
9) a) Se necesita
   b) Hay
   c) Se puede
   d) Hay que
   e) Vale la pena
   f) Hace falta

Pages 96-97: The Passive, Subjunctive and Imperative

1) a) N/A
   b) fue creada por
   c) N/A
   d) será pintado por
   e) fue vista por
   f) son protegidos por
   g) N/A
   h) fue visitado por
   i) N/A
   j) N/A
2) a) ganad**o**
   b) escrit**os**
   c) construid**a**
   d) comid**as**
   e) enseñad**a**
   f) elegid**o**
3) a) iv
   b) v
   c) i
   d) ii
   e) iii
4) a) venga
   b) seas
   c) haga
   d) vayas
   e) tenga
   f) vaya
5) a) tiene
   b) sea
   c) vengas
   d) va
   e) haga
6) a) ¡Canta!
   b) ¡Abre!
   c) ¡Haz!
   d) ¡Sé!
   e) ¡Da!
   f) ¡Aprende!
   g) ¡Di!
   h) ¡Mira!
   i) ¡Ven!
   j) ¡Habla!
   k) ¡Ten!
   l) ¡Sal!
7) a) Termina
   b) Ve
   c) Pon
   d) Juega
8) a) ¡Llámale!
   b) ¡Dime!
   c) ¡Lávalo!
   d) ¡Cómela!
9) a) Tomad
   b) Servid
   c) Dejad
   d) Escoged
   e) Subid

Foundation Speaking Questions — Mark Scheme

It's very difficult to mark speaking questions yourself because there isn't one 'right' answer for most questions. To make it easier to mark, record your answer and use a dictionary, or get someone who's really good at Spanish to mark how well you did. Use the mark schemes below to help you, but bear in mind that they're only a rough guide. Ideally, you need a Spanish teacher who knows the Edexcel mark schemes well to mark it properly.

Read aloud (12 marks)

The read aloud task is divided into two parts. There are 8 marks available for reading the text aloud, and then 4 marks are available for answering the two compulsory questions.

Marks	Pronunciation
7-8	Pronunciation is generally clear and comprehensible. Any lapses have little or no impact on the message.
5-6	Pronunciation is sometimes clear and comprehensible. Lapses occasionally make the message unclear/difficult to understand immediately.
3-4	Pronunciation is occasionally clear and comprehensible. Lapses sometimes cause the message to break down.
1-2	Pronunciation is limited in clarity. Lapses often cause the message to break down.
0	No rewardable material.

Marks	Responding to the questions
2	Response fully communicated.
1	Response partially communicated with some ambiguity.
0	Does not meet the standard required for 1 mark.

Role play (10 marks)

In the role play, you'll be marked on how accurately you respond to spoken language. There are 2 marks available for each of the five tasks in the role play (10 marks in total).

Marks	Responding to the questions
2	Response fully communicated.
1	Response partially communicated with some ambiguity.
0	Does not meet the standard required for 1 mark.

Picture task (28 marks)

The picture task is broken up into three sections. 8 marks are available for your response to the content of the photo on the card, whilst 4 marks are available for answering the compulsory questions and 16 marks are available for the conversation.

Picture description task (8 marks)

Marks	Responding to the stimulus
4	You address two or more bullet points. Your ideas are consistently developed. Your response is generally comprehensible.
3	You address two or more bullet points. There is some development of ideas. You response is comprehensible in some parts.
2	You address one or more bullet points. Your ideas are occasionally and briefly developed. Some parts of your response are comprehensible.
1	You address one or more bullet points. There is little or no development of ideas. Limited parts of your response are comprehensible.
0	No rewardable material.

Marks	Grammar and Vocabulary
4	You use some variety of relevant vocabulary and grammar. Your use of language is generally accurate.
3	You use occasional variety of relevant vocabulary and grammar. Your use of language is sometimes accurate.
2	You use a limited variety of relevant vocabulary and grammar. Your use of language is limited in its accuracy.
1	You use minimal variety of relevant vocabulary and grammar. Your use of language is minimal in its accuracy.
0	No rewardable material.

Compulsory questions (4 marks)

There are two marks available for each question. If you only give a one-word answer, the maximum you can get for that question is one mark.

Marks	Responding to the questions
2	Response fully communicated.
1	Response partially communicated with some ambiguity.
0	Does not meet the standard required for 1 mark.

Conversation (16 marks)

Marks	Responding to the questions
10-12	You give some relevant responses to questions, developing your ideas with some extended sequences of speech. Your response is generally comprehensible.
7-9	You give occasional relevant responses to questions, developing your ideas with occasionally extended sequences of speech. Your response is comprehensible in some parts.
4-6	You give limited relevant responses to questions, with limited development of ideas and brief responses. Limited parts of the response are comprehensible.
1-3	You give minimal relevant responses to questions, with little or no development of ideas and very brief responses. Isolated parts of the response are comprehensible.
0	No rewardable material.

Marks	Grammar and Vocabulary
4	You use some variety of vocabulary and grammatical structures with occasional complex language. You show generally successful use of past, present and future tenses and generally accurate language.
3	You use occasional variety of vocabulary and straightforward grammatical structures. You show some successful use of past, present and future tenses and some clear and accurate language.
2	You use limited variety of vocabulary and straightforward grammatical structures. You show some limited use of past, present and future tenses and limited accuracy with language.
1	You use minimal variety of vocabulary, using short words and phrases in isolation. You show minimal success with past, present and future tenses and minimal accuracy with language.
0	No rewardable material.

Higher Speaking Questions — Mark Scheme

Read aloud (12 marks)

The read aloud task is divided into two parts. There are 8 marks available for reading the text aloud, and then 4 marks are available for answering the two compulsory questions.

Marks	Pronunciation
7-8	Pronunciation is consistently clear and comprehensible. Any lapses have no impact on the message.
5-6	Pronunciation is clear and comprehensible. Any lapses have minimal impact on the message.
3-4	Pronunciation is generally clear and comprehensible. Any lapses have little or no impact on the message.
1-2	Pronunciation is sometimes clear and comprehensible. Lapses occasionally make the message unclear/difficult to understand immediately.
0	No rewardable material.

Marks	Responding to the questions
2	Response fully communicated.
1	Response partially communicated with some ambiguity.
0	Does not meet the standard required for 1 mark.

Role play (10 marks)

In the role play, you'll be marked on how accurately you respond to spoken language. There are 2 marks available for each of the five tasks in the role play (10 marks in total).

Marks	Responding to the questions
2	Response fully communicated.
1	Response partially communicated with some ambiguity.
0	Does not meet the standard required for 1 mark.

Picture task (28 marks)

The picture task is broken up into three sections. 8 marks are available for your response to the content of the photo on the card, whilst 4 marks are available for answering the compulsory questions and 16 for the conversation.

Picture description task (8 marks)

Marks	Responding to the stimulus
4	You address all three bullet points. Your ideas are consistently developed. Your response is easily comprehensible.
3	You address all three bullet points. Your ideas are frequently developed. Your response is comprehensible.
2	You address two or more bullet points. Your ideas are generally developed. Your response is generally comprehensible.
1	You address two or more bullet points. There is some development of ideas. Your response is comprehensible in some parts.
0	No rewardable material.

Marks	Grammar and Vocabulary
4	You use a wide range of relevant vocabulary and grammar. Your use of language is consistently accurate.
3	You use a variety of relevant vocabulary and grammar. Your use of language is mostly accurate.
2	You use some variety of relevant vocabulary and grammar. Your use of language is generally accurate.
1	You use occasional variety of relevant vocabulary and grammar. Your use of language is sometimes accurate.
0	No rewardable material.

Compulsory questions (4 marks)

There are two marks available for each question. If you only give a one-word answer, the maximum you can get for that question is one mark.

Marks	Responding to the questions
2	Response fully communicated.
1	Response partially communicated with some ambiguity.
0	Does not meet the standard required for 1 mark.

Conversation (16 marks)

Marks	Responding to the questions
10-12	You give consistently relevant responses to questions, developing your ideas throughout with consistently extended sequences of speech. Your response is easily comprehensible.
7-9	You give frequently relevant responses to questions, developing your ideas with frequently extended sequences of speech. Your response is comprehensible.
4-6	You give some relevant responses to questions, developing your ideas with some extended sequences of speech. Your response is generally comprehensible.
1-3	You give occasional relevant responses to questions, developing your ideas with occasionally extended sequences of speech. Your response is comprehensible in some parts.
0	No rewardable material.

Marks	Grammar and Vocabulary
4	You use a wide range of vocabulary and grammatical structures with frequent complex language. You show consistently successful use of past, present and future tenses and consistently accurate language.
3	You use a variety of vocabulary and grammatical structures with some complex language. You show frequently successful use of past, present and future tenses and accurate language.
2	You use some variety of vocabulary and grammatical structures with occasional complex language. You show generally successful use of past, present and future tenses and generally accurate language.
1	You use occasional variety of vocabulary and straightforward grammatical structures. You show some successful use of past, present and future tenses and some clear and accurate language.
0	No rewardable material.

Foundation Writing Questions — Mark Scheme

Like the speaking questions, it's difficult to mark writing questions yourself because there are no 'right' answers. You ideally need a Spanish teacher who knows the Edexcel mark schemes to mark your answers properly. Each of the writing tasks has a different mark scheme.

Photo Question (8 marks)

For this question, you're required to write four sentences to describe a photo. There are 2 marks available for each of the four sentences (8 marks in total).

Marks	Responding to the stimulus
2	You clearly communicate the relevant information in a sentence or clause.
1	You partially communicate the relevant information in a sentence or clause.
0	No rewardable material.

14-mark Writing Question

For this question there are three compulsory bullet points. There are 9 marks available for 'Responding to the stimulus' and 5 marks for 'Grammar and vocabulary'.

Marks	Responding to the stimulus
7-9	You address all three bullet points. Some of your ideas are developed. Most of your response is comprehensible.
4-6	You address two or more bullet points. A limited number of your ideas are developed. Some parts of your response are comprehensible.
1-3	You address one or more bullet point. Little to no ideas are developed. Few parts of your response are comprehensible.
0	No rewardable material.

Marks	Grammar and vocabulary
5	You use some variety of vocabulary and phrases. You use simple grammatical structures with some variety, and some linking of sentences with conjunctions. You use some accurate language, with mostly minor errors.
3-4	You use a limited variety of vocabulary and phrases. You use simple grammatical structures with limited attempts at variety, and limited linking of sentences with conjunctions. You use limited accurate language; errors occur, some of which may be major.
1-2	You use minimal variety of vocabulary and/or phrases in isolation, with minimal use of simple grammatical structures, which are likely to be repetitive. There is minimal accuracy in your language, with frequent errors both major and minor.
0	No rewardable material.

18-mark Writing Question

For this question there are four compulsory bullet points. There are 13 marks available for 'Responding to the stimulus' and 5 marks for 'Grammar and vocabulary'.

Marks	Responding to the stimulus
11-13	You address all four bullet points. You frequently develop your ideas. Most of your response is comprehensible.
8-10	You address three or more bullet points. You develop some of your ideas. Your response is generally comprehensible.
5-7	You address two or more bullet points. Your ideas are occasionally and briefly developed. Some parts of your response are comprehensible.
1-4	You address one or more bullet point. You add little to no extra detail to your ideas. Limited parts of your response are comprehensible.
0	No rewardable material.

Marks	Grammar and vocabulary
5	You use some variety of vocabulary and grammatical structures, with some extended sentences and occasional complex language. You generally use the past, present and future timeframes successfully. You generally use accurate language, with some minor errors and an occasional major error.
3-4	You use an occasional variety of vocabulary and grammatical structures, occasionally with extended sentences. You sometimes use the past, present and future timeframes successfully. You use some accurate language, mostly with minor errors and some major errors.
1-2	You use a limited variety of vocabulary and grammatical structures, and short, simple sentences. You use the past, present and future timeframes with limited success. You use a limited amount of accurate language, with frequent major and minor errors.
0	No rewardable material.

18-mark Writing Question

For this question there are four compulsory bullet points. There are 13 marks available for 'Responding to the stimulus' and 5 marks for 'Grammar and Vocabulary'.

Marks	Responding to the stimulus
11-13	You address all four bullet points. You frequently develop your ideas. Your response is comprehensible.
8-10	You address three or more bullet points. There is some development of ideas, and your response is generally comprehensible.
5-7	You address two or more bullet points. There is occasional, brief development of ideas, and some parts of your response are comprehensible.
1-4	You address one or more bullet point. You add little to no extra detail to your ideas. Limited parts of your response are comprehensible.
0	No rewardable material.

Marks	Grammar and Vocabulary
5	You use some variety of vocabulary and grammatical structures with some extended sentences and occasional complex language. You show generally successful use of past, present and future tenses, and your language is generally accurate.
3-4	You use occasional variety of vocabulary and grammatical structures with occasional extended sentences. There is some successful use of past, present and future tenses, and some accurate language.
1-2	You use a limited variety of vocabulary and grammatical structures with short, simple sentences. You show limited success in using past, present and future tenses, and limited accuracy in language.
0	No rewardable material.

22-mark Writing Question

For this question there are four compulsory bullet points. There are 17 marks available for 'Responding to the stimulus' and 5 marks for 'Grammar and Vocabulary'.

Marks	Responding to the stimulus
14-17	You address all four bullet points. You consistently develop your ideas. Your response is easily comprehensible.
11-13	You address all four bullet points. You frequently develop your ideas. Your response is comprehensible.
8-10	You address three or more bullet points. There is some development of ideas, and your response is generally comprehensible.
5-7	You address two or more bullet points. There is occasional, brief development of ideas, and some parts of your response are comprehensible.
1-4	You address one or more bullet point. There is limited development of ideas, and limited parts of your response are comprehensible.
0	No rewardable material.

Marks	Grammar and Vocabulary
4-5	You use a wide variety of vocabulary and grammatical structures with frequent extended sentences and complex language. You show consistently successful use of past, present and future tenses, and your language is consistently accurate.
2-3	You use some variety of vocabulary and grammatical structures with some extended sentences and complex language. There is some successful use of past, present and future tenses, and generally accurate language.
1	You use occasional variety of vocabulary and grammatical structures with occasional extended sentences and complex language. You show occasional success in using past, present and future tenses, and some accuracy in language.
0	No rewardable material.

Listening Transcripts

You can find printable versions of the Listening and Speaking transcripts on the CGP RevisionHub — go to cgpbooks.co.uk/fiesta.

Section One — General Stuff

Listening Track 1 — p.3

3) **M2:** El cumpleaños de mi tío es el veintiocho de octubre y el de mi prima es el dos de diciembre. En junio comienzo a buscar los regalos, pero no compro nada hasta agosto. Para las fiestas, normalmente mi familia y yo tomamos el almuerzo juntos al mediodía. Luego bailamos hasta tarde. Mi familia se reúne en mi casa porque es más fácil que ir a un restaurante. Pero preferiría celebrar mi cumpleaños al aire libre en el parque.

Listening Track 2 — p.3

4a) **M1:** El mes pasado, quería ir a Madrid porque mi amiga estaba enferma. Compré un billete para un vuelo que salía a las seis de la mañana. Sin embargo, había tanto tráfico en la carretera que perdí el vuelo. Luego intenté coger el tren, pero cuando llegué a la estación descubrí que no quedaban billetes. Como todavía no he podido viajar a Madrid, he enviado unas cartas a mi amiga.

4b) **M1:** La semana que viene, tengo nuevos planes para visitar a mi amiga. Voy a viajar en avión y el billete costará ciento treinta y dos euros. También buscaré un hotel cerca del aeropuerto porque así no tendré que viajar muy lejos la mañana del vuelo. Si todo va bien, llegaré a Madrid al mediodía y estaré en el hospital a las dos menos cuarto.

Listening Track 3 — p.5

3) **F1:** ¡Buenos días! Podéis venir a la biblioteca desde las ocho de la mañana y estará cerrada a las seis. Al lado de la puerta, hay un mapa que muestra dónde se encuentran los servicios. Si no sabéis qué libro buscáis, puedo recomendar uno. Abajo hay un café que sirve té y café gratis.

Listening Track 4 — p.6

2) **F2:** ¿Me puede dar más información sobre la ciudad?
M2: Claro. Debe visitar el palacio histórico porque tiene jardines muy bonitos. Una actividad guay para las tardes es ver espectáculos de flamenco. Me encanta verlos en varios sitios. También es posible encontrar comida increíble en los restaurantes.

Listening Track 5 — p.7

3) **F1:** Para el desayuno, normalmente como pan y tomo agua fría. La prefiero a la leche. De vez en cuando bebo té verde, pero bebo café todos los días. En general, me gusta la carne, sobre todo las hamburguesas. Odio el pescado, y no lo puedo comer sin ponerme enferma. ¡Es terrible! Me gustan los pasteles porque están muy ricos. Intentaré comer menos chocolate porque no es muy bueno para la salud.

Section Two — Identity and Relationships with Others

Listening Track 6 — p.8

2) **F2:** ¿Elena?
F1: Vivo con mi madre y su marido. Pronto tendrá un bebé y tengo ganas de ser hermana mayor. Creo que necesitamos una casa más grande.
F2: ¿Malek?
M2: Mi abuelo necesita nuestra ayuda en casa porque ahora tiene que usar más su silla de ruedas. Entonces, mi tía vivirá con nosotros desde el verano. Ella trabaja en un hospital.

Listening Track 7 — p.9

3) a) **M1:** Mi <u>hermana</u> <u>mayor</u> está <u>embarazada</u>*.
b) **M1:** Estoy <u>emocionado</u>* de <u>conocer</u> a mi <u>sobrino</u>*.
c) **M1:** Me llevo bien con mi hermano gemelo.
d) **M1:** Somos los menores en nuestra familia.
e) **M1:** Nacimos en México hace quince años.
f) **M1:** Estoy orgulloso de mi identidad latina.

Listening Track 8 — p.10

1) **M2:** Quiero tener el pelo rubio porque está muy de moda, pero tengo el pelo negro y corto. Mis padres no llevan gafas, pero yo sí. Los tres tenemos los ojos azules y somos muy altos.

Listening Track 9 — p.12

2) **F1:** ¿Andrea?
F2: Mis padres tienen una fiesta enorme cada Nochevieja. Siempre hay mucha comida y bailamos hasta tarde.
F1: ¿Javier?
M1: Tengo ganas de celebrar porque en octubre mi hermana se casará con su novio. Han invitado a mucha gente.
F1: ¿Luis?
M2: Desafortunadamente no puedo tener una fiesta de cumpleaños hoy. Estoy enfermo, entonces me quedaré en cama.

Listening Track 10 — p.13

3) **F2:** Finalmente he decidido una fecha para la fiesta. Será el 22 de julio — cuatro días después de mi cumpleaños. Quiero una fiesta pequeña porque el año pasado había demasiada gente y costó un montón. No obstante, mi novio quiere invitar a su familia entera y me he puesto muy nerviosa. Pedí un hermoso pastel de un comercio local y espero recibirlo a tiempo.

Section Three — Healthy Living

Listening Track 11 — p.14

2) **F2:** Hace unos meses, mi hija menor dejó de tomar el desayuno porque se preocupaba de su figura. Eso me puso nerviosa y quería apoyarla. Después de discutirlo, buscamos información juntas sobre el tema. Descubrimos que muchos científicos creen que empezar el día con el desayuno tiene varias ventajas. Para mí, lo más fundamental es comer una variedad de alimentos, como fruta, huevos y pan. En el futuro, tomaremos el desayuno en familia para ayudar a mi hija.

Listening Track 12 — p.15

4) **M1:** Me encantan los postres fríos. Por ejemplo, en el verano siempre tomo helado. También me gusta tomar bocadillos para el almuerzo. Normalmente son de queso, pero estoy intentando comer más comida vegana.

Listening Track 13 — p.17

3) **F1:** Mi hombro no está roto, pero me duele mucho. Para ayudar con este problema, tomo tabletas cada día. También intento hacer más actividades relajantes. Desafortunadamente, esto significa que no puedo jugar al vóleibol.

Section Four — Free-time Activities

Listening Track 14 — p.18

1) **F2:** Me gusta escuchar música cuando voy al colegio a pie o en autobús, pero no puedo escucharla en clase. Cuando estoy estudiando, prefiero escuchar la música rock porque necesito un ritmo fuerte.

Listening Track 15 — p.18

2) **F1:** El nuevo cine abrirá en el centro comercial este viernes. Tu visita será una experiencia extraordinaria. Gracias a la nueva tecnología, las imágenes de las películas son perfectamente claras. Si tienes hambre, podrás comprar bocadillos y helados.
Sólo durante este fin de semana, tenemos precios especiales, con entradas baratas para todos.

Listening Track 16 — p.20

2) **M2:** Me encantan las historias y personajes, pero encuentro las historias reales aburridas. Conocí a mis amigos en un club de lectura y leemos juntos mucho. También hay muchos puntos positivos de la lectura. He aprendido que es relajante y puede ayudar a la gente a dormir.

Themes 1 and 2 — Mixed Practice

Listening Track 17 — p.24

5a) **M1:** Me encanta <u>leer</u> las <u>revistas</u>.
5b) **M1:** Escribir historias es muy interesante.

Listening Track 18 — p.26

2a) **M1:** ¿Sasha?
F1: Tengo problemas con el pie. No me duele demasiado, pero a veces es difícil correr. Entonces tengo que hacer ejercicio en la piscina.

2b) **M1:** ¿Jalil?
M2: Tomo unas tabletas cada noche para mi espalda. Me duele mucho y la medicina me ayuda a dormir.

Listening Track 19 — p.27

4) **F2:** Hace cinco años mi madre se casó con mi padrastro y ahora tengo un hermanastro menor. Como es muy joven, no hablo con él a menudo, pero me llevo perfectamente con mi hermana mayor. Vivimos en la misma ciudad que mi tía pero en barrios distintos. Ella y mi madre son amigas cercanas y mi tía me hace reír mucho. Pero mi madre es mi modelo de conducta porque es muy trabajadora y no es demasiado estricta.

Listening Track 20 — p.29

3a) **M2:** Montaba en bicicleta cuando tuvo que evitar un coche rápido. Desafortunadamente, sufrí unas heridas. Me rompí la pierna derecha y me corté la otra en la carretera cuando me caí de la bicicleta. Me duele cuando estoy de pie y por lo tanto utilizo una silla de ruedas y tengo que quedarme en cama durante mucho tiempo. Sin embargo, el médico me ha enseñado unos ejercicios que debo hacer también. En dos semanas iré al hospital para comprobar si me recupero bien.

3b) **M2:** Mientras he estado en cama, mi abuela me ha comprado una revista que me gustaba, pero no la he disfrutado mucho porque soy mayor ahora. Me gusta mi propia compañía, pero estar tanto tiempo solo me puso triste. No pude ir ni al colegio ni a ver a mi banda. Sin embargo, vino a verme a casa para animarme. Dentro de unas semanas, debería poder moverme más. Entonces, el médico me ha recomendado ir a la piscina porque el agua reduce la presión sobre mi pierna. Apreciaré un futuro en que puedo estar mucho más activo.

Section Five — Places in Town

Listening Track 21 — p.32

2) **F2:** Vivo con mis padres en una casa pequeñita en el centro de la ciudad. Está en una zona muy moderna, pero me gustaría vivir en una casa más grande porque no tenemos mucho espacio. El sábado pasado, mis padres fueron a ver una casa en otro barrio y les gustó mucho.

Listening Track 22 — p.34

1) a) **M1:** Mi <u>ciudad</u> tiene <u>muchos</u> bares.
b) **M1:** Me gusta <u>visitar</u> el <u>observatorio</u>*.
c) **M1:** La <u>plaza</u> principal es <u>gigante</u>*.
d) **M1:** Siempre hay algo que hacer.
e) **M1:** Mañana quiero ir al mercado.

Listening Track 23 — p.35

3) **F2:** ¿Paula?
F1: Los parques en mi barrio son buenos pero no hay muchos edificios nuevos. Creo que necesitamos más tiendas.
F2: ¿Malek?
M2: En el centro de mi ciudad se puede visitar un café guay. A menudo voy a un cine en la zona sur.
F2: ¿Daniel?
M1: Vivo en el campo y es tranquilo. Pronto van a abrir un supermercado aquí. Será útil pero yo preferiré comprar de tiendas locales.

Section Six — Environmental and Social Issues

Listening Track 24 — p.38

2) **M1:** Vivo en España y aquí hace más sol que antes. También en algunas regiones cae mucha nieve, pero hay menos nubes y viento. Tenemos que hacer más para proteger nuestros bosques. Yo prefiero ayudar al medio ambiente limpiando los espacios verdes.

Listening Track 25 — p.40

2) **F2:** Un instituto está luchando contra el hambre. Si un alumno llega sin haber comido, podrá pedir el desayuno. También, las doctoras del hospital han aceptado una oferta para recibir el mismo salario que sus compañeros. Finalmente, la policía busca a una mujer que toma bicicletas de jardines. Si alguien tiene información, ponte en contacto con la policía.

Section Seven — Social Media and Technology

Listening Track 26 — p.42

2) **F2:** Por las tardes, uso Internet para buscar información para hacer mis deberes. Es muy útil para comprar regalos también porque hay muchas opciones. En este momento estoy triste porque alguien entró en mi cuenta de compras en línea. Quiero tener más responsabilidad y proteger mi información. Entonces, me aseguraré de que cada contraseña sea segura.

Listening Track 27 — p.44

2) **F1:** Me gustaría saber cómo usar la aplicación.
M2: Vale. Chateas con otra gente por mensajes directos. También puedes subir fotos para tus seguidores. Recibir comentarios negativos puede ser un problema, pero hay la opción de parar a otras personas de escribirlos en tu cuenta.

Listening Track 28 — p.45

4a) **M2:** ¿Javier?
M1: Creo que una gran ventaja de las redes sociales es que lo hacen fácil organizar fiestas con mis amigos. Sin embargo, diría que en las redes sociales es irritante mantener todos los contactos que tengo. El otro día envié un mensaje a alguien por accidente.

4b) **M2:** ¿Gaby?
F1: Hago búsquedas en mis cuentas en línea de lugares interesantes que puedo visitar. Así encuentro sitios muy preciosos. Por otro lado, alguna gente no habla mucho en la vida real, debido a que desea pasar la mayoría de su tiempo en las redes sociales.

Themes 3 and 4 — Mixed Practice

Listening Track 29 — p.47

4) **F2:** El reciclaje es esencial. Reciclo mi ropa a menudo y siempre reciclo mi plástico. Mi familia prepara comidas con verduras del jardín. También tenemos muchas flores para ayudar a los animales locales.

Listening Track 30 — p.50

1) **M2:** Jugar en mi portátil es maravilloso porque puede bajar contenido rápidamente. Mi familia tiene una radio. Es moderna pero barata, y ya dejó de funcionar. Como no puedo usarla, escucho música en mi móvil. Normalmente mi amigo y yo vemos una película los sábados, pero este sábado empezaré a ver una nueva serie con él. Sigo a alguien que crea contenido en línea y ha subido un vídeo de él jugando a un juego nuevo. Lo veré solo el domingo.

Listening Track 31 — p.52

1a) **F2:** ¿Amira?
F1: Vivir con compañeras me permite gastar menos dinero comparado con vivir sola. Lo que me molesta es que algunas no hacen ninguna tarea.

1b) **F2:** ¿Jorge?
M1: Vivo con mi primo y compartimos la responsabilidad de cocinar, lo que nos cuesta a ambos menos dinero. Lo irritante de vivir con él es cuando tiene a sus amigos en el piso hasta una hora tarde.

1c) **F2:** ¿Sebastian?
M2: Me gusta vivir con mi familia porque puedo hablar con alguien sobre mi día cuando vuelvo a casa. Sin embargo, creo que no hay suficiente espacio para todos nosotros.

Listening Track 32 — p.54

5a) **F1:** Voy a hablar sobre la diferencia enorme entre los ricos y los pobres. Los ricos no tienen que preocuparse por el dinero mientras los pobres no tienen suficiente dinero para cuidar de sus familias. En mi opinión, necesitamos bajar el precio de la comida, la ropa y las otras cosas que todos necesitan para vivir. Si estos productos esenciales cuestan menos dinero, la gente podrá vivir sin grandes dificultades.

5b) **F1:** Quiero hablar también del delito porque ha aumentado mucho en mi región en los últimos cinco años. En mi pueblo, hay dos grupos de jóvenes que han pintado varios edificios en el centro. Además, han roto las ventanas de unos comercios y los dueños están muy enfadados. La comunidad intenta tomar acción legal contra estos grupos. Sin embargo, ha sido difícil descubrir sus identidades.

Section Eight — School

Listening Track 33 — p.56

1) **F2:** Entre todas mis asignaturas, mi favorita es el inglés. También me gusta hacer ejercicio, pero no disfruto de la educación física. El equipo deportivo es viejo y el campo es demasiado pequeño.

Listening Track 34 — p.57

5) a) **M2:** El <u>gimnasio</u> en mi <u>colegio</u> es <u>estupendo</u>*.
b) **M2:** Encuentro las ciencias muy prácticas.
c) **M2:** El <u>plazo</u> para <u>entregar</u> el <u>ensayo</u>* es estricto.
d) **M2:** Soy consciente de mi comportamiento en clase.

Listening Track 35 — p.58

2) **F1:** Odio las reglas de mi instituto porque, en mi opinión, no son justas. Tienen que cambiar. Además, no me gusta el uniforme que debemos llevar porque no es cómodo, especialmente la corbata. Encuentro mis clases difíciles, pero mis compañeros me ayudan mucho. Entonces, tengo que hacer más deberes.

Section Nine — Future Opportunities

Listening Track 36 — p.60

2) **F1:** Me gustaría ser policía. ¿Qué necesito saber?
F2: Muy bien. No se necesita tener una carrera para hacer el trabajo. Recibirías una formación aquí. Las horas de trabajo pueden ser largas y a veces es necesario trabajar por la noche. Pero es un buen trabajo porque podrías ayudar a tu comunidad.

Section Ten — Travel and Tourism

Listening Track 37 — p.63

3) **F1:** Estoy de vacaciones en Buenos Aires. Me quedo en un hotel muy moderno que está cerca del parque. Mi habitación es cómoda y tiene una vista al mar. Hoy quiero comprar recuerdos para mi familia.

Listening Track 38 — p.64

2) **F2:** Muchos turistas van inmediatamente al museo de arte, pero pienso que primero deberías visitar el palacio porque está en el centro. Hay un castillo cerca pero dentro de unas semanas cerrará. Luego recomendaría coger un barco para ver mejor la ciudad. Puedes bajar a una plaza grande y allí hay un mercado excelente. Vende recuerdos pero es famoso por sus churros. Cerca de la plaza podrás encontrar mapas de la ciudad.

Listening Track 39 — p.65

4) **M2:** El Día de los Muertos es una fiesta importante de México y se celebra el primer día de noviembre. En esta sala, hay fotos que se tomaron hace un siglo. Las personas llevaron trajes como parte de la fiesta y las tiendas vendieron alimentos especiales. Estas costumbres todavía se practican hoy. Durante las celebraciones, la gente ofrecerá regalos a los miembros muertos de las familias.

Themes 5 and 6 — Mixed Practice

Listening Track 40 — p.67

3) **F1:** Cádiz será perfecto para vuestro próximo destino de vacaciones. En primavera no hará demasiado calor, pero todavía se puede disfrutar del sol. O podéis venir en febrero y participar en el Carnaval. Durante esta fiesta histórica, la gente local baila por las calles. También podéis disfrutar de pescado rico y bebidas típicas de la región.

Listening Track 41 — p.68

5) **M2:** Me gustaría ser doctor en el futuro. Puede ser cansado porque las horas son largas, pero el salario es bueno. Primero necesito estudiar una carrera en la universidad. Ahora busco plazas en hospitales para ganar experiencia después del verano.

Listening Track 42 — p.70

3) **F1:** Hola, soy la jefa aquí. Debéis recordar que está prohibido llevar zapatillas de deporte en la oficina. Podéis comenzar el día entre las ocho y media y las nueve y media. La oficina cierra a las siete. Podéis coger días de descanso si estáis enfermos. Durante todo el año, la compañía pagará los desayunos.

Listening Track 43 — p.71

5) **F2:** Recientemente, alguien en mi clase tuvo miedo de hablar con otros. Quería hacer algo para ayudar a las personas que están solas en mi colegio. Decidí organizar un club social que se reúne a la hora del almuerzo. Los alumnos pueden comer y descansar en un espacio tranquilo.

Listening Track 44 — p.71

6) **F1:** ¿Hugo?
M1: Estoy de vacaciones en la costa. Creo que la vista desde mi habitación es increíble. La cama no es cómoda y ahora me duele la espalda.
F1: ¿Luis?
M2: Estoy de viaje en la ciudad. Estoy disfrutando de la comida del hotel. Hay una piscina pero pienso que es muy pequeña.

Listening Track 45 — p.74

4) **M1:** Al final de mis estudios, no quiero ir a la universidad. Preferiría hacer un trabajo práctico. Me gustan mucho los coches, entonces podría aprender a arreglarlos. Sin embargo, mi madre dice que debería conseguir un título. Ella trabaja como policía pero le encantan las ciencias y su sueño siempre era ser científica. Ir a la universidad me permitiría tener un salario mejor. Para mí el dinero que gano no me importa tanto como la felicidad.

Speaking Transcripts

You can find printable versions of the Listening and Speaking transcripts on the CGP RevisionHub — go to cgpbooks.co.uk/fiesta.

Section One — General Stuff

Speaking Track 1 — Read aloud — p.6

Intro: Please read the text.

1) ¿Qué te gusta hacer en tu tiempo libre?
2) ¿Qué piensas de las películas?

Section Two — Identity and Relationships with Others

Speaking Track 2 — Read aloud — p.10

Intro: Please read the text.

1) ¿Qué te gusta de tu personalidad?
2) ¿Cuál es tu opinión sobre casarse?

Section Three — Healthy Living

Speaking Track 3 — Role play — p.16

Intro: You are at the doctor's surgery and you are talking to the doctor. The doctor will speak first.

1) Buenos días. ¿Cómo puedo ayudarle?
2) Vale. ¿Qué tipo de ejercicio hace usted para estar en forma?
3) Muy interesante. Y ¿piensa que tiene una dieta sana?
4) Muy bien. ¿Tiene algún otro problema de salud?
5) De acuerdo. ¿Tiene una pregunta? *(Now answer the question they ask.)*

Section Four — Free-time Activities

Speaking Track 4 — Role play — p.21

Intro: You are at the leisure centre in Madrid, and you are talking to an employee. The employee will speak first.

1) Buenos días. ¿En qué puedo ayudarle?
2) Muy bien. Y ¿qué días quiere venir?
3) Vale. ¿Cuál es su opinión de los deportes?
4) Bueno. ¿Hay un deporte que quiere practicar?
5) Muy interesante. ¿Tiene una pregunta? *(Now answer the question they ask.)*

Themes 1 and 2 — Mixed Practice

Speaking Track 5 — Picture task — p.25

Intro: Describe the picture.

Picture 1:

1) ¿Qué te gusta hacer con tus amigos?
2) ¿Cómo es un buen amigo o una buena amiga?

Picture 2:

1) ¿Cómo prefieres celebrar tu cumpleaños?
2) ¿Qué piensas de pasar las fiestas con la familia?

Unprepared Questions:

1) ¿Quién hay en tu familia?
2) ¿Cuál es tu actividad favorita para hacer con la familia o los amigos?
3) ¿Qué vas a hacer para celebrar Nochevieja este año?

Speaking Track 6 — Read aloud — p.28

Intro: Please read the text.

1) ¿Qué te gusta hacer por la tarde?
2) ¿Cuál es tu opinión de vivir con mucha gente?

Speaking Track 7 — Picture task — p.30

Intro: Describe the picture.

Picture 1:

1) ¿Qué piensas de los deportes?
2) ¿Qué actividades deportivas hiciste la semana pasada?

Picture 2:

1) ¿Qué piensas de los conciertos?
2) ¿Qué música escuchaste el fin de semana pasado?

Unprepared Questions:

1) ¿Cuál es tu pasatiempo favorito?
2) ¿Cómo fue la última vez que fuiste a un restaurante?
3) ¿Qué tipo de ejercicio vas a hacer este fin de semana?

Section Five — Places in Town

Speaking Track 8 — Read aloud — p.33

Intro: Please read the text.

1) ¿Qué te gusta hacer donde vives?
2) ¿Cuál es tu opinión sobre tu comunidad?

Speaking Track 9 — Role play — p.36

Intro: You are in a tourist information centre, and you are talking to an assistant. The assistant will speak first.

1) Hola. ¿En qué puedo ayudarle?
2) Bueno. Y ¿dónde se encuentra su hotel?
3) Muy bien. Y ¿qué tiempo prefiere?
4) Vale. Y ¿qué piensa del pueblo?
5) Muy interesante. ¿Tiene una pregunta? *(Now answer the question they ask.)*

Section Six — Environmental and Social Issues

Speaking Track 10 — Picture Task — p.41

Intro: Describe the picture.

Picture 1:

1) ¿Qué piensas de trabajar en comunidad?
2) ¿Qué hiciste para mejorar tu barrio el año pasado?

Picture 2:

1) ¿Qué te gusta hacer por otras personas?
2) ¿Qué hiciste el mes pasado para ayudar a tu comunidad?

Unprepared Questions:

1) ¿Qué piensas de las diferencias entre grupos sociales?
2) Háblame de un problema que ha afectado a los jóvenes en el pasado.
3) ¿Qué debería cambiar en la sociedad en el futuro?

Section Seven — Social Media and Technology

Speaking Track 11 — Read aloud — p.42

Intro: Please read the text.

1) ¿Qué te gusta hacer en Internet?
2) ¿Qué piensas de las redes sociales?

Themes 3 and 4 — Mixed Practice

Speaking Track 12 — Picture task — p.48

Intro: Describe the picture.

Picture 1:

1) ¿Qué piensas de las videoconsolas?
2) ¿Cómo usas la tecnología en casa?

Picture 2:

1) ¿Qué haces con tus amigos en línea?
2) ¿Cuál es tu opinión sobre las redes sociales?

Unprepared Questions:

1) ¿Cuánto tiempo pasas en Internet?
2) ¿Qué hiciste en tu móvil ayer?
3) ¿Cómo vas a usar la tecnología la semana que viene?

Speaking Track 13 — Role play — p.50

Intro: You are at a shopping centre in Spain, and you are talking to an employee at the information desk. The employee will speak first.

1) Buenos días. ¿Cómo puedo ayudarle?
2) Muy bien. Y ¿qué le gustaría comprar?
3) De acuerdo. Y ¿por qué visita usted la región?
4) Vale. ¿Qué piensa de la zona local?
5) Interesante. ¿Tiene una pregunta?
   (Now answer the question they ask.)

Speaking Track 14 — Role play — p.53

Intro: You are in an electronics shop in Spain and you are talking to a member of staff. The member of staff will speak first.

1) Buenos días. ¿Cómo puedo ayudarle?
2) De acuerdo. ¿Qué características le gustaría?
3) Muy bien. Y ¿para qué va a utilizar el aparato?
4) Vale. ¿Tiene una pregunta?
   (Now answer the question they ask.)
5) ¿Tiene otra pregunta?
   (Now answer the question they ask.)

Speaking Track 15 — Read aloud — p.54

Intro: Please read the text.

1) ¿Qué te gusta hacer para ayudar a tu comunidad?
2) ¿Cuál es tu opinión de dar dinero a causas sociales?

Section Eight — School

Speaking Track 16 — Read aloud — p.57

Intro: Please read the text.

1) ¿Qué te gusta estudiar?
2) ¿Qué piensas de tu colegio?

Section Nine — Future Opportunities

Speaking Track 17 — Picture Task — p.60

Intro: Describe the picture.

Picture 1:

1) ¿Quieres ir a la universidad? ¿Por qué?
2) ¿Qué hace un/a buen/a estudiante?

Picture 2:

1) ¿Cuál es el trabajo de tus sueños?
2) ¿Qué piensas de trabajar en un centro comercial?

Unprepared Questions:

1) ¿Qué trabajo hace un miembro de tu familia?
2) ¿Qué estudiaste en el instituto ayer?
3) ¿Te gustaría ser profesor(a) en el futuro? ¿Por qué?

Section Ten — Travel and Tourism

Speaking Track 18 — Role play — p.63

Intro: You are in a hotel and you are talking to the receptionist. The receptionist will speak first.

1) Buenos días. ¿Cómo puedo ayudarle?
2) De acuerdo. ¿Qué transporte tomará?
3) Muy bien. Y ¿tiene una pregunta?
   (Now answer the question they ask.)
4) Y ¿qué piensa del hotel?
5) Vale. ¿Tiene otra pregunta?
   (Now answer the question they ask.)

Themes 5 and 6 — Mixed Practice

Speaking Track 19 — Picture task — p.66

Intro: Describe the picture.

Picture 1:

1) ¿Qué piensas de los museos?
2) ¿Qué actividades hay para los turistas en tu región?

Picture 2:

1) ¿Qué te gusta visitar durante un viaje?
2) ¿Adónde te gustaría ir de vacaciones?

Unprepared Questions:

1) ¿Qué festival cultural quieres ver?
2) ¿Qué hiciste durante tus vacaciones del verano pasado?
3) ¿Qué vas a hacer durante tus próximas vacaciones?

Speaking Track 20 — Role play — p.69

Intro: You are at a tourist office in Spain and you are talking to an employee. The employee will speak first.

1) Buenos días. ¿Cómo puedo ayudarle?
2) Muy bien. ¿Cuándo quiere ir?
3) Vale. ¿Dónde está su hotel?
4) De acuerdo. ¿Qué tipo de transporte prefiere?
5) De acuerdo ¿Tiene una pregunta?
   (Now answer the question they ask.)

Speaking Track 21 — Picture task — p.73

Intro: Describe the picture.

Picture 1:

1) ¿Qué piensas de la tecnología en tu instituto?
2) ¿Cómo usaste la tecnología en clase recientemente?

Picture 2:

1) ¿Cómo son las instalaciones de deporte en tu instituto?
2) ¿Qué hiciste en tu última clase de educación física?

Unprepared Questions:

1) Para ti, ¿cuál es la mejor manera de estudiar?
2) ¿Qué deberes recibiste la semana pasada?
3) ¿Qué harás después de terminar tus estudios del instituto?

SPEQ42